W9-BYP-631

PREPARING FOR SPIRITUAL DIRECTION

PREPARING FOR
SPIRITUAL DIRECTION

Jean Laplace, S.J.

Translated by
John C. Guinness

FRANCISCAN HERALD PRESS
1434 West 51st Street • Chicago, Illinois 60609

Text Copyright renewed, 1975, *by*
DONALD C. MacDONALD

Text: Twenty-eighth Printing
Illustrations: Nineteenth Printing

Preparing for Spiritual Direction by Jean Laplace, S.J., copyright ©
1975 by Franciscan Herald Press, 1434 West 51st St., Chicago, Illinois
60609, originally published as *La Direction de Conscience ou Le
Dialogue Spirituel,* Paris, Maisone Mame, 1965. First English edition
published by Herder & Herder as The Direction of Conscience, New
York, 1967. Present edition by arrangement with original publishers.

Library of Congress Cataloging in Publication Data:

Laplace, Jean, S.J.
    The direction of conscience.

    Reprint of the 1967 ed. published by Herder & Herder, New York.
    1. Conscience. I. Title.
BV4615.L313 1975   241'.1   74-17135
ISBN 0-8199-0550-X

March 25, 1975

Imprimi potest: Jean Villain, S.J., Vice Provin-
cial; *Nihil obstat:* Brendan Lawlor, Censor
Librorum; *Imprimatur:* ✠ Robert F. Joyce,
Bishop of Burlington, September 13, 1966.

MADE IN THE UNITED STATES OF AMERICA

Contents

Foreword, by John Carroll Futrell S.J.   11
Introduction   13

Chapter One:
The Direction of Conscience and the Pastoral Ministry   21
1. Some Criticisms of Spiritual Direction   23
2. The Objectives of the Spiritual Dialogue   26
   EDUCATION TO FREEDOM   27
   SPIRITUAL DISCERNMENT   29
   THE RECOGNITION OF EVENTS   33
   A PERSONAL RELATIONSHIP   35
   ADAPTATION, NOT UNIFORMITY   40
   FOCUS ON THE REAL WORLD   43
   A SOURCE OF ASSURANCE   44
3. Spiritual Direction as a Priestly Task   45
   COUNSEL IN TRUST AND FREEDOM   45
   THE ROLE OF THE PRIEST   47
   CHARISMA AND DISCRETION   51
4. Spiritual Direction and the Renewal in the Church   54

Chapter Two:

The Nature of the Spiritual Dialogue   56

1. The Natural Foundations of the Spiritual Relationship   57
2. The Spiritual Dialogue and the Natural Order   61
3. Spiritual Fatherhood and the Life of the Spirit   66

   THE RELATIONSHIP IN ITS BEGINNINGS   70

   THE DEVELOPMENT OF THE RELATIONSHIP   78

   THE RELATIONSHIP MUST BE OPEN   80

   THE RELATIONSHIP AND THE PERSON   88

   THE ANALOGY OF THE RELATIONSHIP   91

Chapter Three:

The Formation of the Spiritual Director   94

1. Knowledge of the Spiritual Life   96
2. Openness to Others   104
3. Spiritual Experience   118

   DOCILITY IN THE HOLY SPIRIT   119

   PURITY OF HEART   120

   THE PEACE OF GOD   124

   LARGENESS OF HEART   128

4. Aptitude and Capability   129

Chapter Four:

The Kinds of Spiritual Direction   134

1. The Person and What He Can Bear   134
2. Occasional Direction   140
3. Collective Direction   143
4. Direction by Correspondence   145
5. Permanent Direction in Some Cases   147

   YOUTH   147

   VOCATIONS   149

CONTENTS

THE FAMILY   152
WOMEN   158
RELIGIOUS   159
PRIESTS   162

Chapter Five:
The Psychology of the Directed   167
1. The First Meetings   167
2. The Qualities of the Directed   175
   INTELLIGENCE   175
   TRANSPARENCY   179
   A SPIRIT OF FAITH   184
   A SPIRIT OF SIMPLICITY 186

Conclusion   188

Foreword

This reprinting of Fr. Jean Laplace's book on spiritual direction is an event of great importance for the Church at the present time, and the publishers deserve our sincere gratitude. The very fact that this book was unobtainable for some years and now is being reprinted points up the rapid changes in attitudes among priests, religious, and laity during the past decade.

The last years of the 1960's were a time when many persons considered that God was dead, that prayer was irrelevant, and that the spiritual life could be lived within a totally secular dynamic. Spiritual direction definitely was not in vogue. When the euphoria of that era passed so rapidly into disillusionment with the self-sustained efforts of man to achieve peace on earth, economic prosperity, and the secular paradise, the rediscovery of the transcendent of the early 1970's emerged and with it a great revival of prayer and of interest in the spiritual life. Spiritual direction began to be sought seriously once again, and various programs were initiated for the training of good spiritual directors.

Although an increasing number of excellent articles on spiritual direction and even a few worthwhile books about it have appeared during recent years, there is still great need of really solid works grounded in experience and clearly and concretely expressed to be available to people desiring to become good spiritual directors or actually engaged in giving direction.

In my own courses and workshops on spiritual direction, I have always recommended Fr. Laplace's book as simply indispensable.

It remains, in my opinion, the best work in English on the topic. The book is the fruit of many years of prayerful reflection by Fr. Laplace on his own experience as one of the most sought after and esteemed spiritual directors in France. Every page of the book has the concreteness of life, of real spiritual dialogue with real people seeking to clarify their experience of God.

Fr. Laplace describes the qualities necessary in a good director, above all that the director be a person of deep prayer and of spiritual experience in order to help others grow in the Spirit. He also gives excellent insights about how to profit from spiritual direction, so that his book is as useful for the directed as for the director. He gives very practical advice about the dialogue of direction, about the relationship of spiritual direction to psychological counselling, and about helping the directee to grow constantly in freedom and in authentic spiritual discernment. His understanding of the deep personal love the director must have for the directed, based, once more, on his own loving qualities as a director, is clear and moving. If you wish to give good spiritual direction to a person, "You must love him to start with" (p. 62).

Perhaps the best description of a spiritual director is that one must be "a loving, listening presence." Reflection on the wisdom put by Fr. Laplace into this book will enable us to learn how to love much more, to listen with greater sensitivity, and to make ourselves ever more present to the other. I hope that this new printing of *Preparing for Spiritual Direction* will reach the hands of all spiritual directors and all those seeking good spiritual direction.

John Carroll Futrell S.J.

Introduction

THIS book is addressed first of all to priests, and it must be admitted that among the clergy spiritual direction does not have a good press. It gives rise to sympathetic laughter, and finds itself relegated to the junk-rooms where we put away statues made at the end of last century. The overburdened apostle of the twentieth century does not know what to do with this luxury instrument, useful to fishermen with rod and line, but unemployable for those great sweeps of the net that he would now like to make into the mass. New times, new methods.

All the same, the question cannot be quite as simple as that. At any meeting of priests, one has only to turn the conversation onto the subject for everyone to prick up his ears. A listener who had not been forewarned would soon conclude from the aggressiveness coloring some of the comments that spiritual direction is one of those scapegoats upon which are loaded many an unadmitted discontent. Who is there who has not regretted, feeling the insufficiency of his own training, that he did not meet with a real spiritual director on his road?

Nor are laymen indifferent to the question. How many of them, and from all sorts of environments, complain that they get no help from a priest as soon as they begin to talk to him about their inner lives! "There is a lot being said today," they observe, "about the new role of the layman. But we wish priests would think a little more about the layman's right to a spiritual life."

Priests are often concerned at the disaffection of the faithful, and sometimes the best of them, towards the sacrament of penitence. Is it lack of faith alone that is responsible? Are they always aware of the profound disappointment they cause when a layman who has been hoping for a word of illumination or encouragement is met only with embarrassment, clumsy phrases, a feeling of hurry or a ready-made exhortation? What are we to say of the scandal of an education that calls itself Christian, but from which a young man can emerge without ever having had a deep contact with a priest? Undoubtedly these questions call for an answer.

But do we in fact know what we are talking about? The notion of spiritual direction is hardly more confused among its detractors than among its adepts. Strive as one may for cool judgment, the impression remains that criticisms and eulogies alike are being showered on a caricature. It seems that many people complain of it only because they are expecting something from it that it was never intended to give, or because, like so many religious realities, its development is suffering from sclerosis. What is the reality? We have the picture of a foggy and unexplored domain that people have a bad conscience about not knowing, but are afraid that if they venture in they will be made fun of.

A priest who intends to go into the subject tries to see himself in the part he will have to play, since he will usually be the one who must take on the role of director. Feeling himself incompetent, and yet wanting to do the best he can, he asks for a manual, a pastoral guide, written by those who have the practice for the use of those who have not. Besides, such a manual would gladden the hearts of its users, faithful, religious, or priests, who are anxious for spiritual direction themselves. They think it would tell them, rather like those formal examinations of conscience for people who are in doubt about the best way of confessing, what can properly be expected of a director and how he should be employed.

For our own part, we have grave doubts about the value of such a book. The art of direction cannot be learned from manuals, any more than the art of being the father of a flock. To be a father, one has first to be a man; to be a director, one has first to be spiritual. Guides are useful, but only if you already have some experience of what an expedition is. Even the best courses of initiation, which many priests complain that the seminaries do not give, only succeed in creating the illusion of knowledge if the person who is following them does not already know for himself the inner life that is being spoken about.

Now life, whether it is that of the Spirit or that of the Church, cannot be reduced to formulas or set out in synoptic pictures. Before making over-all plans or tracing the limits of frontiers, it is necessary to face reality and, out of the respect that one has for it, discover its laws. The reality of spiritual direction, like all living realities, must be examined in its movement, which is at the same time both simple and complex.

We shall, therefore, first try to assign a place to spiritual direction in the living reality of the Church and the individual. This will be the subject of the first two chapters. When direction has been seen as one of the multiple manifestations of the life of the Spirit in the Church, leading a person on to spiritual maturity, we shall be able to clarify in the two following chapters some of the laws of its exercise in general, and also in particular cases. We must be careful not to forget that for the best of directors, as for the best of fathers, there always remains the unknown factor: the freedom of the person he is addressing. This we shall speak of in the final chapter.

There will be nothing new in these pages for the scholar, who may find them too simple, or for the practical man, who may judge them to be too complicated. We do not intend to elaborate a theological justification for spiritual direction, or to lay down laws for the director's guidance, or to offer advice or issue warnings. We shall attempt an analysis in depth and in its exercise of this special experiment which it is given to certain people to make in a relationship of spiritual help. In it, two human beings meet. Both of them are caught up from the start in something greater than themselves. What is the meaning of the bond which is established between them? How must they both behave in order to preserve the truth of the relationship, as much in its beginnings as on the summits of the spiritual life?

Now that our object has been defined, it is easy to guess the spirit in which this book should be read. The danger would lie in wanting to make it fit into preconceived frameworks, or searching it for recipes for one's apostolate. It would be far better if the reader could allow himself to be shaken up by it. What we are hoping from him, in this attempt to give to spiritual direction as it has always been practiced by the Church its pastoral, spiritual, Christian, and human coördinates, is that he will allow himself to be patiently worked upon by the many questions that his reading may suggest to him, personalizing them at the same time out of his own experience. Only in this way will he find the fraternal support and stimulation that he has a right to expect from it.

Read from this angle, this book is not addressed only to priests. Certainly it should help them, we may dare to hope, in their more certain and joyful exercise of a delicate ministry. But we like to think that the layman—religious or faithful—will find it no less profitable. In the Church, a spiritual life is no man's endowment, and in the elaboration of his own ideal he should thus be better placed to understand what he has a right to expect from the ministrations of the priest.

These pages, finally, are the echo of many different experiences, and of exchanges of views between priests and laymen. It is obviously impossible to say except in general what they owe to those personal conversations in which a director tries to "follow" his charge and allow himself to be formed by him. In this domain, one always receives more than he gives.

We have retained the expression "spiritual direction," although many do not like it, and no doubt with good reason since it suggests something different from the reality that it is trying to express. But it is traditional; and so as not to bewilder those who are in the habit of using it, we have kept it. Also it is a mark of our bond with the tradition that the word conceals. We prefer, however, the term "spiritual dialogue," especially as there are many who would rather speak of a counsellor than of a director.

PREPARING FOR SPIRITUAL DIRECTION

CHAPTER ONE

The Direction of Conscience
and the Pastoral Ministry

SET against all the tasks confronting the pastoral ministry in
these days, spiritual direction pales by comparison and seems like
a reality answering the needs of another age. Dispiriting memories are perhaps all that a priest has left from his interviews at the
seminary with the one who was conventionally referred to as his
director. Since then, he has had no director, or is still looking
for one. If he worries about the question when he is in retreat, it
is really to give himself a good conscience about a practice that he
was formerly taught to regard as important. He knows very well
that in a year things will be just as they are now. After all, he
has a confessor, whom he sees regularly. What more could he
expect from a director?

He does not know the answer for himself. How should he
know it for the others, colleagues or laymen, who come to ask
him for help? He is embarrassed. The exhortations of the confessional seem to him to be quite enough. Apart from bits of
practical advice, drawn from his memories or his reading, he does
not see what a spiritual dialogue could consist of. He gets out of

it by saying that he is not a specialist. But the question goes on worrying him. He has the feeling of a call to which he cannot respond.

With others, the embarrassment takes another form: it becomes aggressive and goes over to the attack. Direction as it is now practiced has had its time, they say. It no longer corresponds with existing needs, and that being so, it cannot form part of apostolic activities. A priest should not be concerned with it. He has better things to do today, and must concentrate on numbers. If a few Christians come and ask him about direction, he looks at them kindly and protectively and suggests that they should evolve. Belonging to a group, engaging in concrete action, will give them more and better help than all the spiritual direction in the world.

We could go on adding to the picture; but further touches could do no more than express under one form or another the profound uneasiness curently felt by the best and most apostolic of priests. They have the greatest difficulty in finding a place for spiritual direction in the midst of their crowding activities.

We must first try to analyze the causes of this uneasiness. What are the criticisms that a priest is tempted to make about spiritual direction? Faced with a criticism, one can always ask whether it does not show ignorance or misapprehension of the reality that is being discussed; but it may also be concealing a disappointment or expressing a desire. It is from this angle that we should look at the criticisms. We shall take them as an opportunity for putting spiritual direction to the question. From the examination, we may hope that it will emerge rejuvenated and purged of its caricatures, so that the priest of the twentieth century can accept it as one of the most authentic forms of his pastoral ministry.

1. SOME CRITICISMS OF SPIRITUAL DIRECTION

The first criticism levelled against spiritual direction is that, rather like religious obedience in certain eyes, it does not respect the freedom of the individual. Habituating the person directed to questioning the smallest details and submitting himself in everything to the decisions of another, it would be suitable only for minors, or would keep others in a state of prolonged minority.

This criticism is joined to a second which has been voiced to more than one spiritual director: that in the course of the ages, by giving direction a precise form, spiritual life has been mechanized. It has become simply a matter of fidelity to exercises known in advance and consigned to a list of regular practices. Included under this heading is the reflection of a priest: "Has spiritual direction in the course of the centuries taken the place of the Holy Spirit in the early days of the Church? If we are finding disaffection on the subject today, is it not because we are rediscovering a sense of the action of the Spirit in the Church?" It can hardly be a matter of astonishment that the modern generation, which is so sensitive to everything that touches its freedom, should be tempted to throw overboard an exercise that has in any case become too institutionalized, that appears to be indifferent to freedom, and that no longer answers a real need. It is left to those for whom restraints remain necessary; but they themselves cannot use it as a means of helping men to whom respect for freedom is the first condition of all dialogue.

A further cause of uneasiness is the danger that seems to threaten everything concerned with religious feeling—that of illusion. Trained in psychological disciplines, our contemporaries have become highly sensitive on this point. Is it not evident that

23

many interior states formerly submitted to the judgment of a director properly belong to the realm of psychological analysis? The true life of faith must not be confused with this world of feelings. And spiritual direction here meets with the same criticism as does the examination of conscience: that it tends to fix our attention on such feelings to an exaggerated extent.

In face of the progress of psychology, the proper domain of spiritual direction seems therefore to become smaller and smaller. All religious feeling is suspected of being nothing but a subjective experience, the result of psychological conditioning. In the end, we begin to ask ourselves anxiously what will be left of the interior world. Must we not further admit that those who talk about spiritual direction today emphasize what it is not, put people on their guard against the dangers, but scarcely say what it is?

The reply to this criticism, that there exists a spiritual world which is independent of the psychological one, only causes further uneasiness: this so-called "pure spiritual" seems to be very unreal. Undoubtedly, every priest knows that there is a spiritual life, and he is as concerned for himself about it as are his elders. But he is concerned also that it seems to many people to be a closed world, indifferent to everyday events and the miseries of mankind. He is sensitive to all that his contacts with the world have revealed to him about the value of the daily round and the most humble tasks, and this sense of actuality he does not want to lose. Spiritual books speak to him in a language that he no longer understands. He finds in them nothing but abstract and edifying considerations that people nowadays are sick of. Is this the insipid and out-of-date language that he is going to meet in spiritual conversations? There are too many spiritual fathers who, rightly or wrongly, give him the impression of being remote and other-worldly. He wants to avoid that kind of eccentricity at all costs. He cannot accept the idea that a spiritual life should take no account of actuality, whether it is that of world history or the history of the individual.

Moreover, he has become particularly sensitive to this danger, which he knows to be a real one, as a result of all that he has gained from the community sense of our times. And here is a new cause for uneasiness. Direction being primarily a dialogue between man and man, it seems to him that even if it avoids all the dangers we have mentioned, it will be tainted with a vice which he fears above all others: that of individualism.

Rightly or not, it appears to him that many of the advantages that were formerly expected to result from direction can now be derived from the life of the group, and even with a truth and fullness that private dialogue cannot reach. The latter remains fixed on the interests of the self; the group awakens its members to all sorts of concerns that entail the giving of the self. In particular, the life-review, a practice adopted by a large number of religious or priestly groups, has become in many people's eyes the modern form of spiritual direction. Here, the dichotomy between the spiritual life and the community or apostolic life at once disappears. Personal life becomes directly engaged in the life of the community.

A final cause for uneasiness attaches to the above criticisms: spiritual direction implies the existence in the Christian community of privileged members, to the detriment of a mass incapable of attaining the heights to which direction leads. The priest is afraid that the care he is giving to a few may cut him off from the majority, to whom he is bound by his ministry and whose language he wants to speak. He is afraid that his contact with the spiritually minded might cause him to adopt ways of speaking and acting that, without his even being aware of it, would set him at a distance from the rest of mankind.

The reader is free to discover for himself the ambiguities hidden under these various arguments. Whatever they are, they are still an expression of the feelings of a priest in regard to traditional methods of direction, and basically they compose his sense of uneasiness about any form of ministry not understood by the masses and appearing to isolate him from them. Rather than finding in his way of looking at things the manifestations of an adolescence not yet outgrown, let us take it as an expression of his solicitude that no man should be excluded from the message of Christ. Every criticism reveals a secret need. Let us start from that so as to define our direction. It will be a means of breaking free the reality that lies hidden under the sclerosis of words and habits. The priest, and every Christian with him, will more easily understand that a direction which seeks to help the individual in his spiritual life is, whether given or received, one of the manifestations that are most necessary to the pastoral activities of a priest today.

2. THE OBJECTIVES OF THE SPIRITUAL DIALOGUE

We are going to say what takes place in the dialogue of direction, and what points it must touch upon if it is to bring the help that is to be expected from it. These points, as we shall see, are simple. They are the very ones which give the Christian life its adult character: respect for freedom, the life of the Spirit, the sense of individual vocation, personal relationships, the variety of the grace of God. Direction can be defined as the help that one man gives to another to enable him to become himself in his faith.

Education to Freedom

It would certainly be a gross error to conceive the dialogue of direction as teaching given by a master to his disciple. Even if it were concerned with freedom, such teaching would not answer to the deepest desires of the recipient, who is not asking about the nature of freedom, but what he must inwardly do to be able to serve God with a free heart.

We must affirm that spiritual direction is not possible except with a person who already has a certain sense of freedom. Or rather—for how many adolescents who do not know that they are, must be restored to their unhappy lot!—its first objective is to confront a person with the degree of freedom that he has, and help him to grow in it. This dialogue is sometimes long and painful, if someone has to accept the evidence that he cannot do the great things he wants to do, because he has omitted to lay the foundations and because he does not know himself. This is the story of so many vocations, so many generous plans that have no natural bases.

Let it be said at once that the object of this dialogue is not of a purely natural order, even if its primary aim is the formation of freedom. If it teaches a person to know and accept himself, it is with the certainty that no spiritual progress can be accomplished by ignoring or running away from his natural endowments. When that object has been recognized on both sides from the beginning, it forms the first real step in the life of faith. The point of application is natural, but the object is docility to the Holy Spirit on the basis of this concrete nature.

What is not to be tolerated is for a person to make direction an excuse for avoiding decisions of his own. I am doing what my director tells me, so I have nothing to worry about. Everything is falsified by this affirmation. Direction becomes domination, and an abuse of confidence, of people who do not want to disturb their minority. There are many who have to recognize that they were expecting direction to be something quite different from what it is; but what it cannot be in any sort of way is a substitute for lack of will.

There are directors who are convinced at the beginning of the truth of this principle, but seem to forget it afterwards. They do not care to maintain those whom they direct in this climate of freedom. On the contrary, having an acute sense of their charge, and bearing with anguish the souls that have been entrusted to them, they are like those directors whom Surin speaks of in his *Dialogues spirituels,* who truly want to help souls, but who wish, he says, "at all costs to establish their own practices in souls, and do not make themselves sufficiently dependent on the Spirit of God." We know priests whose pupils, especially if they have strong personalities, leave them after some time. Grateful though they may be for the training they received at first, which was vigorous and well-founded, they later come to admit that under the severe discipline, useful as it may have been at the start, they feel unable to breathe.

What such directors lack is a concrete sense of that freedom which is a condition of the life of the Spirit. Spiritual as they may be, they have not yet learned to follow the Spirit of God in the directing of souls that He has committed to their care.

We see, then, that the dialogue of direction, whether it is envisaged in its early stages or at a later point in the spiritual life, cannot develop unless it respects the freedom of the other. Direction is not an arbitrary matter; it must pay attention to the personal development and the possibilities of an individual. The service of God requires free hearts, and the spiritual life cannot flourish unless account be taken of the inmost forces that move each one of us, so that they become responsive to the action of the Holy Spirit. It is for us to dispose ourselves, by developing our freedom and purifying our hearts, to receive the always unforeseeable gifts of grace.

Spiritual Discernment

Often when these unforeseeable movements of grace are considered, there will come to many minds another question: Are we developing our freedom only to have it submitted to that world of uncertain feelings where illusion and error lie in wait for us?

There have always been good people in the Church who have been afraid that the awakening of a personal life in the believer's heart would also stir up the mirage of the feelings. They think that the life of faith requires nothing more than an austere fidelity. It arouses less enthusiasm, but seems to be more sure in its results. Today, as a result of the progress of psychology, their apprehensions have taken a different form. This spiritual discernment in which we insist that the whole nature of direction is enclosed, what else is it but a perceptible reëcho of the religious life? Would it not be hazardous to claim to be in the presence here of another world?

It must be observed, however, that the discernment of spirits is at least as old as the apostles. It is, if we are to believe St. Paul and St. John, the sign of a developing spiritual life. "It is my prayer," says St. Paul, "that your love may abound more and more, with knowledge and all discernment, so that you may approve what is excellent" (Phil. 1, 9-10). "Do not believe every spirit," says St. John, "but test the spirits to see whether they are of God" (1 Jn. 4, 1). There, beyond doubt, we have the germ of what we call spiritual direction. The apostle's task is to teach the faithful not to put their trust, without testing them, even in the holiest gifts—apostolate, prophecy, teaching, the gift of miracles or of administration: in their exercise must be recognized the signs of the Spirit, which are "love, joy, peace, patience, kindness, goodness, faithfulness, gentleness, self-control" (Gal. 5, 22–23). Simply the holiness of an undertaking is not a sufficient guide to assure us that we are doing God's will: the way in which we set about it can spoil everything. "I belong to Paul," says one. "I belong to Apollos," says another (1 Cor. 3, 4). Such intransigence shows that the Christian who talks like this is still only a child, a being of flesh, subject to discord and jealousy (1 Cor. 3, 1–3). He has not submitted his activity to the superior wisdom of the Spirit (1 Cor. 1–3). Moreover, is not Scripture, taken as a whole, an initiation into discernment between true and false salvation, so that the Christian may come through it to recognize in the disconcerting twists and turns of human history the "power and the wisdom of God" (see 1 Cor. 1, 18–25), and to glory in the cross of Christ alone? (See Gal., esp. 6, 14.)

For St. Paul, then, as for the apostles, there is a whole life of the Spirit in us, whose outward manifestations in ourselves or in the community must be carefully distinguished from all the others, to which they bear only a superficial resemblance. Every Christian who is growing in the faith must, with the help of the Church, become capable of this discernment. If not, he is still at the rudimentary stage of faith, receiving children's milk, and far from the perfect man whose moral sense has been "trained by practice to distinguish good from evil" (Heb. 5, 14). The adult Christian is one who both submits himself to the unpredictable freedom of the Spirit, and knows "of what Spirit he is."

The first centuries of our era witnessed the flowering of a true doctrine of spiritual direction, springing from the certitude of the life of the Spirit and the necessity, while we live in the flesh, of discerning its action. We are referring here to the writings of the Fathers, and especially those of the Greek Church, concerning directly or indirectly the discernment of spirits.

In this tradition, direction appears essentially on the pupil's side as an outpouring of all his thoughts to his spiritual father, so that in this inconsistent and continuous flood he may learn to "discern the spirits," that is to say, the interior emotions, "suggestions, impulses from within," which come sometimes from God and sometimes from the devil. In this way, as a result of the struggle demanded by discernment, he is able to attain the true freedom of the children of God who are led by the Holy Spirit. In practice, it is not so much a matter of confessing sins or failings as of reaching down to the roots that underlie the sinful act, and of purifying the heart, from which proceeds all that defiles a man (see Mt. 15, 18). This confession, made in simplicity and trust, brings about ·in the one who consents to it a true self-emptying, as we should say in modern terms; but because it is accompanied by frequent recollection of the Lord Jesus who purifies all things, instead of leaving the individual to the solitude of his discoveries, it opens up the depths of the being to him who is its unique and veritable Master, the Spirit who has made us. Naturally, to be efficacious, that is, to be enlightening, the confession must be made to a man of experience. Everyone is therefore invited to choose a father from among the elders, who will become his guide in this new life that he is entering with ardor, but of the perils of which he is ignorant. Thus, in this extremely rich tradition of the East, the outpouring of one's secret thoughts, the choice of a spiritual father on the ground of experience, and the search for spiritual freedom are the essential elements of all direction. Here is a way of action suited to every Christian, be he monk, lay, man or woman, who has it in his heart, in whatever station of life he is called to live, to allow the grace of Christ to manifest in him.

Most certainly, there can be no question of a literal adoption of counsels valid for other times, but we shall find in this tradition a precious heritage of which it is good that we should take account. It is remarkable that another master in direction, St. Ignatius Loyola, should have rediscovered in his rules for discernment, the practice of which he explains in his exercises, the teachings and even the forms of expression, although he had no special knowledge of them, of these great masters of the Christian East.

If there is one point where the dialogue of direction, the nature of which we are attempting to describe, can profit from this spiritual tradition, it is assuredly that of the discernment of spirits. Has there ever been, in the history of the Church, a time of greater ferment than our own? It resembles in this respect the first ages of Christianity or the period of the Renaissance. If, then, on the one hand we do not want to extinguish the Spirit, but if on the other we are anxious not to be carried away by every spirit, never was a dialogue of discernment more necessary. How many there are who mistake for a sense of sin the uneasiness they experience in the face of their own disorder, or the feelings of guilt brought back by certain memories of childhood! Others, ready for any undertaking, accept as inspirations of the Spirit the generous sentiments aroused in them by the love of humanity or concern for their neighbors. To both, dialogue of a spiritual and not just a psychological kind is necessary for light to be shed on an interior world where psychological elements interfere, as we shall explain more fully later, but which cannot be simply reduced to an analysis of that sort.

The Recognition of Events

The dialogue which aims at discernment may engender a fear in someone who is trying to understand its object—the fear he experiences in reading certain spiritual books, of finding himself carried very far from the life of every day. What we should wish is for discernment to be applied not only to those moments of privileged solitude when we meet God in the prayer of the desert, but to everything that makes up the daily warp and woof of our existences. Events, as we say today, are the signs of God. Direction should train us to recognize them.

Now that is precisely what direction claims to do. It is not applied to some reserved domain, but seeks to purify the understanding so that in every gesture, every reaction, every feeling which shows our deeper tendencies and secret resources, we shall be given to see the most perfect way of living a situation. It is a whole man who is thus led to God, a man who has learned never to doubt His love, and who believes that in and through the most unexpected circumstances, God does not cease to call us to Himself (Rom. 8, 28).

The dialogue of direction takes on an exceptional character when we are seeking to discover the will of God for the whole of a life. The problem of vocation has at all times been one of its privileged subjects. But it is a matter of observation that the concern for realism, which must as we insist be the primary aim of every such conversation, at once allows us to frame the question in more objective and more spiritual terms. Vocation, like every call of God, is actually inscribed in the concrete history and interior dynamism of the individual. It is through a study of both of these that we may expect direction to show us the revealing light of God's will, rather than through a sudden revelation, or a wise assessment of the reasons for committing the self to one course or another. The spiritual dialogue that has everyday life for its regular object will allow us more easily to recognize with the passing years the signs God gives us through events, signs which may so easily remain imperceptible to one who is not trained to exercise his insight on them.

Taking up again a favorite theme of the Church Fathers, we can say that the goal of direction is to develop another sense in us by daily exercise. Every Christian has this sense, thanks to his baptism, but many do not realize its existence, and in them it remains inffective, as would the sense of sight in someone who had left it undeveloped through lack of use. Spiritual dialogue attempts to teach us little by little, and in all circumstances, the acuteness of this discernment, and sustains the slow effort of purification that is necessary to reach it.

Such knowledge as this cannot be acquired from all comers, for it is a knowledge of life. It is the endowment of the wise, of those who have followed the example of the writers of the Books of Wisdom, have reflected about existence and have allowed themselves to be taught by it. That is no doubt why spiritual fathers are found among men of ripe age. Of symbolic age, we must add, for there are those among the young who have the wisdom of the old, and there are older men whose experience has taught them nothing. Tradition requires that the priest, whatever his age, should be one whose long contact with God in silence has brought him to reflect about existence, and to look at it with a penetrating eye. Let us hope that too great a hurry for immediate results will not prevent the priest of today from playing this part among his contemporaries. They expect from him not only that he should understand and share their anguish, but that he should bring into the very heart of this anguish the peace and light of the faith by which he lives.

A Personal Relationship

An education to freedom with a view to the spiritual discernment of one's own and other people's lives: why does traditional doctrine suppose that this can take place only in a dialogue of person to person? The question is often asked. The individual character of direction seems, to many, old-fashioned and out of date. They think that the same results could be achieved by group relationships. These offer the advantage that in bending the individual to the demands made by action and by other people, complacency and introversion—the permanent dangers of all individualist pedagogy—can both be avoided.

However it may be in theory, many priests will admit that in practice their spiritual life has gained more in a few months from group living than from years of individual direction. And so, every time that they engage in a dialogue of personal help, they have the feeling that they are wasting their time. Compared with the newer methods of apostolate, the results of direction, real though they may be, seem limited or of little use.

It is to be expected that the evolution of our own time should have a profound effect on our way of living the realities of the spiritual life. The community dimension is an inescapable fact. Not that it did not exist before, in any authentic faith: how can one love God, not loving one's brother? But the evolution and the aspirations of the modern world, the development of the sciences of psychology and sociology, have taught men to live together in a way that they formerly did not. The situation can only hasten the death of individual and bourgeois piety. What remains to be seen is whether the flowering of this new type of spiritual life, more communal in appearance, does not demand just that personal relationship we have been describing, only purified now of the detritus of the past.

The question is whether a human education, whatever its object may be, can achieve this without some previous relationship of person to person. In social life, a man finds his balance and is at ease only to the extent that his parents or teachers have been personally engaged in existence with him. What remains without them an abstract code and a yoke heavy to be borne, becomes with them spontaneous and natural. So, in the order of the Spirit and of Christian life, institutions and the group are necessary to the Christian in order to teach him the law of Christ and make him act out in living the solidarity that binds him to other men. But this social commitment remains empty and formal in the absence of that personal contact which teaches one how to be committed and remain faithful to it.

The dialogue of direction possesses, then, in contrast to the objective order of the institution and the group, that eminently personal character that should belong to all pedagogy. It brings the absolute order within everyone's measure, adapting it to his age, his condition, his proper grace: "Not to limit the law, but to train the capacities of souls to the exigencies of the law." Father Lucien-Marie de Saint-Joseph, whom we have just quoted, goes on to say, "Faith, because it is transcendent, is never actualized in any soul twice in the same identical way."[1] The director is not teaching a new law, but the way of observing it, which is the way of the Spirit. While a preacher remains in the order of the absolute, he, always having a personal aim, knows that what is best in itself is not necessarily, at any given moment, the best for me. Whether it is a matter of choosing a state of life, or the everyday engagements offered to a Christian, he tries to prevent the mistakes of wilfulness, or answers that are given more out of fear or a sense of duty than out of love. He tries to coöperate with the action of the Holy Spirit, whose unction teaches nothing other than what was said by Christ, but who, by bringing remembrance of the inwardness of exterior commandments, makes them light and easy in practice.[2]

Every director has experience of this necessity of interiorization. How many there are who, in accomplishing what they believe to be, or what really is, the will of God, yet remain hard and rigid! They speak of the demands, but forget the sweetness, of the Holy Spirit. They tire out their imitators, and their own efforts can be sustained only to the detriment of their health, their balance and right understanding. Others, lacking the discernment that a guide could give them, are the playthings of illusion or of ill-advised generosity. They fail to see that the ardor they are spending is only a means of concealing from themselves either their own deficiencies or a humiliating situation that they dare not face.

It should be clear that a group cannot begin to fulfill this role. It can reveal an individual's shortcomings, or constrain him to

---

[1] "Etudes Carmélitaines," *Direction spirituelle et psychologie,* pp. 188–189.

[2] See 1 Jn. 2, 20 & 27; Jn. 14, 26; 1 Jn. 5, 4; Mt. 11, 28–30.

admit to himself the secret springs of his actions. But if he has not reached a sufficient level of personal integration, he is often crushed by this revelation and runs the risk of sinking into discouragement. It is one thing to be able to see what one is, but quite another to bear it with gentleness, making the insight a principle of progress. Discernment by all means, but achieved in peace: that is the objective of personal direction.

Such an objective can only be of advantage to a group. Direction will allow the quality of commitment to be purified, will avoid all regimentation, will give adherence a character that is more true, more personal, and more divine. What the individual, left to himself or the law of the group, might accomplish with difficulty, in disorder or anxiety, direction, addressing itself to his most intimate being, will bring him to realize with joy and trust.

All of this is increasingly finding its realization in the practice called the life-review. Many priests are even inclined to say that the life-review is the modern answer to the direction of consciences. However, this kind of thinking does not put matters in their proper perspective, for spiritual direction and the life-review are, in fact, situated on two different levels of life, and we must take this distinction into account if we are to benefit from both. The life-review is situated on the objective level of events in the ordinary life of the world, insofar as these have already been embodied in the work of salvation. It attempts, by examining them in the light of the Gospel, to form the objective judgment that the Christian community should have of them. This is a valuable method for recognizing the presence of God in all reality, even the most profane, for enlarging the individual's viewpoint which always tends to be fixed only on his personal problems, for enabling the group to profit from the reactions of each member and make more palpable its concrete unity in

Christ. But, unless it is wanting to establish spiritual collectivism, it does not avoid the necessity for the individual to harmonize his own ways, his own life, with the common vision. But direction gives the life-review a more intimate and personal bearing, and leads to conclusions which are not within the province of the group. And this in its turn can be only to the group's advantage. We are here on two levels which are not opposed, but which move in opposite ways, to the greater profit of both: the objective and the subjective, the institution and the person. To the extent that everything is given its place, and one is not duped by words, the spiritual life of the individual and that of the group are mutually developed by each.

A priest, apparently wanting to justify his reserve about spiritual direction, one day asked the following question: "Fundamentally, how far does its use go back in the Church?" On condition that we do not try to enclose it in institutions that have their day, its reality has always existed. Even further back than Christ, when he personally educated his apostles before sending them out to preach, we might recall the companies of prophets grouped about a master whose spirit they desired to penetrate, and the repeated counsels of the Books of Wisdom, seeking to form in the one who consented to follow them the "soul of a disciple."[1] We are faced with the fact that the Word is passed on from mouth to ear, and the master who lives by it teaches his disciples its meaning and practice. This way of looking at things is so natural that Our Lord warned of its excesses: "But you are not to be called rabbi by men, for you have one teacher" (Mt. 23, 8). To remain faithful to the use of direction—its forms may vary, but its reality is as old as the life of the Spirit—is simply to remain faithful to the laws of life itself.

[1] Thus Prv. 3, 1. 4. 5, etc.

Adaptation, Not Uniformity

Among the causes of hindrance often mentioned in discussions on the subject of spiritual direction is the kind of selection operated among Christians by the special interests that it implies. The very language it employs would seem the prerogative of a few privileged people, a sort of aristocratic luxury that hardly conforms to the simplicity of the Gospel.

One might certainly observe that the danger threatens any group which, in order to give a special training, tends to limit itself to that. What priest has not had it said to him during his clerical infancy that he was one of the privileged few? Direction cannot escape this limitation.

But the limitation should not make us forget the reality: in the Church, the variety of the grace of Christ; and in each individual, the variety of the moments of grace. As with every life, there is nothing uniform about life in the Holy Spirit. It should not lead a director to treat everyone in the same way. Adaptation, with all its inequalities, is the fundamental rule. St. Paul laid down the principles long ago: they are those that rule the life of the body. It is by diversity in a unifying charity that the body lives and grows. "Each has his own special gift from God, one of one kind and one of another" (1 Cor. 7, 7). This growing in Christ has many degrees, is of many kinds, includes particular charisms and inequalities. There is the Christian who is beginning (see 1 Cor. 3, 1-4), the "engaged spirit," as Mouroux calls him in *The Christian Experience;* and at last there is the spiritual man. Each follows his rhythm. Every Church has its own, that of Rome and that of Ephesus. Through men and down the ages, the Church spreads over the world like a living thing, according to a rhythm at once personal and universal. Here is perhaps one of the greatest difficulties met by a priest, who is himself committed to a work or to a movement, every time that someone comes to him for advice: he is greatly tempted, above all if he is dealing with an exceptional person, to want to project his dreams onto him and enroll him in his special enterprise. But the service of God is not a human work; it is the answer to a particular call. The priest who is a director must help each individual to discover this particularity.

Generally speaking, and we shall often repeat it in the pages that follow, it would not be right to impose direction on everyone, or to think of it in a uniform manner. There are some who would find in it nothing but useless complications. To be reminded of the commandments, to be taught with everyone else, to join in common prayer, to receive their confessor's counsel, faithfully to perform fixed exercises: these will be enough to sustain them in the Christian life. Why ask them to do something that they feel no need to do? It would be useless for them, or at least premature. Let them go their way in peace, simply keeping an openness to the possible calls of God. The function of a spiritual interview would be to confirm them in the road that they are following, and to keep each within the limits of the possible.

But a priest must know how to recognize those who are wanting something more, and must not refuse it to them out of concern for an equalitarianism that has nothing evangelical about it. These are the ones who have achieved a minimum of autonomy, and are beginning to show in themselves a desire for unity. They are to be found in all walks of life. They are neither better nor worse than other people. Simply, they want to live with all their being, and in all the events of their lives, the faith of their baptism. It is a call to discernment that they have in them, and also a need for deep purification and a radical belonging. Spiritual dialogue is a necessity for them, to help them to reach the light and to serve God in peace.

It may happen that there are some among these who are deluded. In asking for help, they are only trying to find themselves, or are tilting at windmills. The director, in talking to someone like this, will have to lead him very gently to understand the illusion he is nursing. If he realizes his mistake, he will have learned from that first discernment to accept himself, to take his life in hand, and to wait for God's hour in a complete realism of faith. A lingering adolescent might be encouraged by such an interview to achieve one day that state of freedom without which a spiritual life is impossible.

The tragedy would be for a priest not to hear the genuine calls, or to smile at them. He would be like the men St. John of the Cross speaks of who, ignorant of the ways of God and the spiritual world, seek to impose their own ways of doing things on all who ask them for advice. If there are any who do not agree with their principles, or suggest that there may be a slightly different point of view, a well-managed or sympathetic smile will allow them to feel how naïve, how complicated, or how unreal they are judged to be.

A respect for the grace that is in everyone, far from leading to the particularism which excludes some and favors others, teaches us to recognize in all men the gratuitous and universal action of God. By developing his particular gift, a man discovers the gift of the Spirit that dwells in him. The outcome of dialogue will be a mutual dependence on the action of the Spirit which is moving throughout the Church. It attains its end to the extent that it makes us each and all aware of the active presence of God in all and each. Far from turning a person inwards on his privileges, it opens him to thanksgiving and to the life of the Church.

Focus on the Real World

The preceding analysis has shown us how easily the words "direction" and "director" can give us a false idea of the reality. Perhaps it would be better to speak of a dialogue of assistance, and of a spiritual counsellor. But these words too can become worn out, if one has not discovered the world that they are intended to evoke.

For the priest who is a director, if the reality of the life of the Holy Spirit in us is not a more real world than the one we see with our eyes, a process of degradation inevitably awaits the help he claims to give. Unable to see in the world of the Spirit a reality that exists of itself, that has its own laws and is not for him to handle as he wishes, the priest may be tempted to look for reassuring and palpable results that have little or nothing to do with the operation of the Holy Spirit. Direction becomes in his eyes a means of checking the progress that has been made, either to acquire a degree of control, or to give someone the assurance of psychological or moral balance, or else to achieve the particular ends of some undertaking.

Director and directed alike, unless they are careful, may become enclosed in the natural satisfaction they feel in the search for a certain kind of virtue or perfection, the attachment to a certain number of practices, or the adherence to some enterprise or movement. There can be no spiritual help unless both of them, in the efforts in which they are engaged, keep their eyes fixed on the virtues of God's word, which alone give the others their supernatural value and keep the heart at the disposal of the Holy Spirit. Without that focus, the help a director seeks to give, by whatever name it goes, inevitably becomes degraded.

A Source of Assurance

If, on the contrary, one is careful to attach himself to the reality underlying the traditional idea of direction, it is no matter if the name changes; the reality will always be felt as a necessity for the Church. The finest Christians, whatever their intellectual or social level, will always seek out those priests who, faced with the supreme choices of existence as with its daily details, will teach them to depend only on God and to submit themselves to the movement of the Holy Spirit, so as to be the more disposed to receive his gifts. No kind of clerical domination, however subtle, is to be expected from priests such as these, for contact with them reveals men who are at peace with themselves. Bending to the vicissitudes of temperaments and of living, never wearied, they penetrate beyond the present situation, helping those entrusted to their care to look to Christ alone for the unity of their lives. They are the true directors.

Why should our generation be deprived of their aid? So many kindly people are living in ways that are impersonal, rigid, and hard. So many are haunted by anxieties and fears. So many among the best are driven by restlessness, try to do everything, and are overwhelmed by the awareness that well-intentioned apostles urge them to have of every situation. So many of the apostles themselves need to learn discernment, so as to be able to serve God with the ardor of quietness. Others, who did not find the help of a good director when they needed it, remain, like children whose parents have neglected them, tied up in their complexes, odd, meticulous, distracted. Perhaps they are no less sanctified, but they give out little or no light. Sound direction would have been a source of assurance for them and of balance, a means of becoming more human and more spiritual. "Direction is a timeless reality," says Irénée Noye, "which contributed to the ascetic effort of the first centuries, to the development of mysticism, to the sanctification of the laity, to the regeneration of the clergy," and is no doubt called "to be of service also to those gifts that the Holy Spirit today is giving to his bride. Is it not in times of searching and of growing that there is need for the discernment of spirits?"[1]

3. SPIRITUAL DIRECTION AS A PRIESTLY TASK

We have spoken of direction until now as of a task normally arising from the ministry of a priest. The priest himself, even if he thinks of it as an out-of-date form of activity in relation to modern conditions of life and apostolate, nevertheless regards it as something, whether old or new, that pertains to him by right. But is this correct? To what extent does it pertain to him?

Counsel in Trust and Freedom

The fact is, spiritual direction does not require the offices of a priest, either historically or theologically. In the early monastic communities, the candidate for the priesthood chose a spiritual father from among the elders to initiate him into the new life that he desired to lead. The father of his choice was not usually a priest. All that was required of the spiritual director was spiritual maturity and experience. This same observation could

---

[1] In *Supplément de La Vie Spirituelle,* no. 34, pp. 251 ff.

also be made of groups of nuns; and it is a matter of record that up until the seventeenth century a number of lay men and women came to be eminently regarded as spiritual directors.

These facts are understandable. It is the whole people of God that must grow spiritually, and all of them in proportion to the gifts they have received must help one another in the building up of the Body of Christ. The task is not exclusively assigned to anyone, but all together, as St. Paul expresses it, must "attain to the unity of the faith and of the knowledge of the Son of God, to mature manhood, to the measure of the stature of the fullness of Christ" (Eph. 4, 13). The things of importance in this mutual building up are the experience and the charisma received; and the priesthood of itself confers neither the one nor the other.

A number of priests have an instinctive understanding of this fact in the confessional, when they are dealing with visiting penitents whose confession seems to require some explanations, or encouragement in the spiritual life. They will often discreetly ask them, "Have you a director who can help you to shed light on this point?" Adding, if necessary, "Do you feel at home with him? Would you like to have a further talk on the subject?" They need say no more than that. The domain of confession is one thing, where the penitent confesses his sin to the priest who has the power to absolve him; quite another is that of direction, where the Christian seeks to understand himself better, so as to reach down to the roots of evil and open himself more deeply to the action of God. For the one, the sacramental power is required; for the other, experience. St. Ignatius, in his "Rules for the Discernment of Spirits," makes this remark on the subject of revealing one's thoughts or temptations: "They should be talked over with a confessor, provided he is a good one, or with any other person who is habituated to spiritual things" (*Spiritual*

Exercises, no. 326). The confessor is certainly not excluded, but if he is being asked for aid and counsel, it is not inasmuch as he confers the sacrament, but inasmuch as he knows. If he does not know, it is better to address oneself to a man of experience, even if he is not a priest.

The fact that the Church forbids the superiors of non-clerical congregations to require inferiors to open their consciences to them, should not mislead us here.[1] What the Church wants above all to preserve is the freedom of choice. She also wants to prevent the real abuses to which such an obligation might give rise. Direction can be profitable only if it is established through a relationship of trust and freedom. It would be wrong if, as an indirect result of this decree, priests were to draw the conclusion that they are sole masters in such matters. That might lead, especially in communities of women, to even greater excesses than those involved in an obligation to expose one's conscience to a superior. The Church is anxious to avoid all domination over consciences, in any place whatsoever, and this includes clerical domination.

The Role of the Priest

Nevertheless, the Christian conscience does instinctively attribute this role to the priest in a special and privileged way, and there is astonishment when the priest shows himself undesirous or incapable of accepting it.

The primary motive for this way of thinking is of a practical nature. More than anyone else, the priest seems to have the necessary competence for the task. A certain amount of human and theological culture is indispensable to warrant the charge of the

[1] Decree *Quemadmodum,* December 17, 1890.

direction of others. It is a safeguard against the notorious dangers of counsels given by uncultured spirits—narrowness, eccentricity, sectarianism, and regimentation. Numerous examples could be given of groups in which life becomes unbearable because of the presence of saintly people, full of good will but with limited ideas. If the priest has received a normal training, it is to be hoped that he will avoid these excesses. Accordingly, we can advance the proposition that although direction may not of itself be the privilege of a priest, it is nevertheless rare for a priest not to be called upon to intervene in the case of an individual who is needing spiritual help. Besides, if we consider the motives that lead us to think in this way, we shall see that the fact of his being a priest is only one of them. Our religious instinct senses that we need to consult a priest, but at the same time that we must choose him well. What we are looking for especially in him is a man of knowledge, religious and experienced.

But there is a deeper motive in this bond between the priesthood and direction, and it is of an ecclesiastical nature. "The mission of directing souls towards perfection appertains to the priest, for he is the rightful mediator prolonging the mediation of Christ and of the Church. . . . Persons not invested with the priesthood may be called to share this mission, provided that the Church, which administers the mediating mission of Christ, invests them with the privilege." This direction is then "exercised in a derived and partial manner, . . . inasmuch as these persons will appear as connected with the priesthood, and with the hierarchy of the Church."[1] In these remarks there are certain points with connections that must be understood in view of assuring a proper balance to the spiritual life of people who feel the need of

[1] Gabriel de Sainte Marie Madeleine, *Dictionnaire de Spiritualité*, cols. 1181-1184.

direction. Undoubtedly, what I require of my director in the first place is that he should be competent thanks to his experience and learning, and that I have been able to choose him freely. This competence I shall not find in every priest, and again I may find it in someone who is not a priest. But if it is truly the perfection of the life of Christ in myself that I am looking for, I can hardly conceive it except in reference to the Church and her hierarchy.

One could, of course, understand in a very general sense this mediating function of the Church which is exercised through the priest. It would be possible to see him within the Christian community as a symbol of the unity of the body of Christ to which every spiritual life aspires, and without which it cannot be a true life.

But would it be right to dissociate to that extent a man's function and his spiritual life, when the function itself has no other end than the sanctification of the people of God? Being invested with a power which aims at the sanctification of all, how could a priest be indifferent to the progress in sanctification of those for whom he is working? The sacrament of penitence, in the measure that it is a personal act of a man in Christ, requires a minimum of direction, and this should at least dispose the Christian to weigh the consequences of his acts. Tradition has certainly understood it in this way. "Auricular confession, as it is now practiced in Catholicism, is born from the need of spiritual direction."[1] One might sometimes even be tempted to think that it had become overdeveloped in that sense, and the fact had been forgotten that it is essentially a sacrament, and therefore an encounter with Christ in the Church which has as its starting point the person that I am. In truth, the very notion of the

[1] *Dictionnaire de Spiritualité,* col. 1207.

priestly ministry becomes withered if we exclude from it the element of direction that it contains. More than any man, the priest who is ordained to the service of the people of God must respond to the spiritual calls of his brothers. Without that, his priesthood would be reduced to a mere set of duties, validly accomplished, but not for the spiritual edification of all.

Let us say that even if, in practice, direction is a charisma that is not given to everyone, and no more to a priest than to the next man, it remains true nonetheless that anyone who by his office in the Church is charged with a ministry that relates him to the hierarchy, is called by that very ministry to operate the discernment of charismas, of which one important aspect happens to be personal direction. No doubt, as H. Denis says, "the hierarchy has no monopoly of the Holy Spirit, and could not conceivably appropriate it. But it has the task of discerning it in a normative fashion. If it turned its back on that task, it would be allowing the community of believers to be tossed about at the mercy of illuminism."[1] It is for the hierarchy to recognize and preserve the charisma, even though it cannot create it. Ultimately, it is the hierarchy that confers its authentication on the spiritual master, for the good of the whole body.

Direction, even when it is exercised by those who are not priests, can in this way be said to participate in the mediating function of the Church.

Certainly, we must not confuse obedience rendered to a hierarchical superior with that shown to a spiritual father. The superior declares the will of God, and can impose it; the director helps to discover it or do it, and imposes nothing. Nevertheless,

[1] "Réflexions sur le sacrement de l'ordre," in *Vocations sacerdotales et religieuses*, no. 227, July, 1964, p. 342.

the docility with which one listens to his counsels, to the very extent that he is recognized by the hierarchy even if he is not himself invested with the priesthood, will reflect the obedience that one gives to all those who exercise this mediating function in the body of Christ.

Charisma and Discretion

While we may affirm that it is normal to expect every priest in the Church to be capable of this dialogue of spiritual aid, we must hasten to add that it is not to be expected of every priest uniformly, since the aptitude for direction is, after all, a charisma.

No doubt we can also say that there is a minimum which every Christian has a right to hope for. Recourse to confession is not to be considered, either on the part of the faithful or on that of the priest, as a quasi-automatic act without any relation to, or bearing on, the dispositions of our hearts or the commitments of our lives. But how one could wish at times for a priest to be discreet about it! His position does not authorize him to resolve everything, or to ask questions about everything. It is not his duty to give me advice, if he does not know me. The embarrassing enquiries, the idle and arbitrary dissertations! The awkward blunders, too! A priest must realize that in helping to shed the grace of Christ on a human life, he must be content to act for a single moment in a story of which he does not hold the secret, and the course of which he must respect.

There are times when he must exercise discretion over what he says; he is there only to do as did the forgiving Christ. Others before him or after him are responsible for the bringing of the necessary help; he intervenes only in passing. There are other cases, on the contrary, in which at the same time as being the minister of grace he must also be the educator who enables its slow workings to be perceived. Then he becomes a director. Either way, he has to realize that in this mediating role which he alone in the Church has the power to perform through the sacraments, he is never dealing with people who have no history and no souls. He must never take advantage of his priesthood to strike out at random. He must be all the more careful not to do so because the person who is coming to him is not concerned with the distinctions that a priest is required to make, but receives his every word as if it were from Jesus Christ himself. The confessional is not to be treated as a means of passing on a priest's favorite ideas or enrolling people in his work. It is at the moment when he is making use in its fullness of the power of Christ that he has most delicately to respect the unforeseeable work of the Spirit.

What we have just been saying becomes especially relevant in a usage, the meaning of which often escapes even the priest who practices it for others or for himself—devotional confession. It is born neither from a need of analysis nor from a desire for pardon. If it where either of these, it would be unhealthy. Rather, it springs both from the intimate knowledge that the light of God gives us of ourselves, and the certainty that, alone, we cannot respond to the demand for purity which it brings. The Christian who feels moving in him that subtle and ineradicable pride which he meets in every action, but which it is impossible for him precisely to avow, can only in his confession make an ardent supplication to the Lord who both knows and changes our innermost beings: Make me a clean heart, O God. Recourse to the sacrament is itself that cry. In the almost continuous harassment by which Satan tries to discourage all effort, to vitiate all progress and kill hope, we return to the very source of life, the blood of Jesus Christ. This kind of confession is not a recital of precise details or past faults, but the avowal of that permanent state of the heart, that confusion of thoughts, that secret evil of which we are more and more aware that we cannot be healed, unless by a conversion which is the work of grace. It is truly in this case that confession forms part of a spiritual life already enlightened by direction, and it is here that the priest must be especially attentive and discreet.

In short, when he is faced with this dialogue that is expected of him, the priest has to preserve the humility of his priesthood. The fact that in one way or another he is participating in the pastoral mission of the Church, must not delude him into thinking that because of this he is himself living out those gifts of which he is a guardian and interpreter. Undertaking such a dialogue, he will require the qualities that go to make both a man and a spiritual being, that combination we shall attempt to describe when we come to draw the portrait of the spiritual director. This is a domain where a Christian may quite rightly expect much of him, yet he does not enter it as into ground that properly belongs to him and where by grace of his condition he might legislate at ease. On the contrary, if he is attentive to the work of the Spirit, he will find himself being schooled by the most humble of those in whom he discovers its wonders. From them, and without their knowing it, he will learn more of the ways of God than from all the books put together.

His experience of the facts will teach him that in the body of Christ all the members complete one another, and none of them is privileged. All are equal in the Spirit, and his priesthood is given to the priest only for the service of the people of God, in the midst of whom he looks upon himself as just one among many.

4. SPIRITUAL DIRECTION AND THE RENEWAL IN THE CHURCH

The evolution of the world today and the impulse given to the Church by the Council have aroused great hopes in the hearts of Christians. But they cannot prevent a vague disquiet from being mingled with their hopes. How are we to make a judicious selection from the legacy of the past? Do we not run the risk, when we weed out the old growth, of pulling up the shoots that are just about to open? This is the kind of anxiety that takes hold of a priest when he is faced with the fact of spiritual direction. Confronted with this, as with many other forms of his ministry, he is bound to question himself about the course that he should adopt.

There is little doubt that he will need more than ever before to take the time to sit down and try to answer these questionings in the sight of God. Direction then will no longer seem to him to be a respectable vestige of past times; set against the aspirations of the modern world, it will appear as a necessity for these days. It is not opposed to any other forms of apostolate; on the contrary, it is in contact with them that it draws from the source of essential rejuvenation. And these in turn will profit from the spiritual discernment which is its distinguishing mark—the discernment which all the newer forms of apostolate, simply because they are so new, most urgently require.

Seen in this light, and in its proper place, direction of conscience, or spiritual dialogue if the term is preferred, once more becomes in the eyes of today's priest an eminently sacerdotal task.

Not giving way to despair in his attempt to master this "art of arts," as St. Gregory the Great called it, it will be enough for him to give himself to all that the work includes, if he has received the call and the charisma for it. He realizes then that the existence of this ministry enables those who come to him, and especially those who are in the service of the Kingdom, to persevere in their right choices, to keep their probity of heart, and to have peace and joy under difficulties. In that, he becomes the collaborator of the Holy Spirit, ensuring that the whole Church, "joined and knit together by every joint with which it is supplied, when each part is working properly, makes bodily growth and upbuilds itself in love" (Eph. 4, 16).

If a priest who has given thought to the present exercise of his ministry does not find himself putting spiritual dialogue on a level with the most important services that he or others can give to Christians today, perhaps it would be good for him to question himself about the quality of his apostolic inspiration. He would find it to be a test by which he could justly evaluate the spiritual worth of his sacerdotal life. Ignoring or despising this form of activity, he would be showing his own lack of the understanding that he claims to have of the mystery of the Church. We are here in the presence of two complementary realities: pastoral work and spiritual direction. Their dissociation can only operate to the detriment of both.

CHAPTER TWO

The Nature of the Spiritual Dialogue

IF priests are showing little belief at the present time in the
value of spiritual direction, it is perhaps, as we have just been
saying, because they have not been able to assign a place to it in
the aggregate of their sacerdotal activities. Also perhaps because
they are ill at ease in face of the subjective reality of living that
this relationship demands. What is a priest's personal attitude
towards those who come to seek his help? What are his own
feelings when he is involved in the new relationships that spring
up between people in one another's presence?

Direction is a dialogue, and, like all dialogue, it implies a
personal relationship between human beings. Given this object,
it calls on the deepest resources of each of them, and brings into
play the whole range of affective contacts. A director, under the
necessity of committing himself, may be seized with panic at the
affective deficiencies that this threatens to reveal to his own eyes
or to another's; he may then refuse the challenge of a deeper
relationship, and take refuge in a conventional attitude, in which
dialogue is accepted as a necessary duty but where neither partner
gives himself without reserve. This kind of abstract and impersonal relationship is quite useless. If it is to meet the expecta-

tions of another, the one accepting it must commit his whole being.

What happens then? What is the nature of the relationship so established? Tradition refers to it as a paternal one, and we commonly speak of spiritual fathers. But the word disturbs our modern sensibilities; we are afraid of imposed authority or of a self-complacent paternalism that prolongs someone else's minority status. Many would rather speak of friendship, of brotherly support, of a helping hand. These words suggest free choice, sharing, a common search that respects the liberties of the participants. In any case, these various ways of speaking, old or new, imply a relationship which, in order to become real, must reach down into the deepest levels of being. Let us try to locate ourselves at that depth, and then decide if we can what name to call the relationship that ensues.

1. THE NATURAL FOUNDATIONS OF
THE SPIRITUAL RELATIONSHIP

We must first attempt to show the extent to which the incipient relationship between director and directed is rooted in the depths of human nature. Everyone is familiar with the dialogues of Socrates, and the warnings he gave to young Hippocrates, who was quite ready to entrust his soul to the first teacher he found, because it was the fashionable thing to do. It is a serious thing, Socrates reminded him, to entrust one's soul to anybody.[1] Socrates himself is the representative in antiquity of the type of man who does not write books, but spends his life in revealing others to themselves: he is a midwife of souls, according to his own ex-

---

[1] Plato, *Protagoras*, 313.

pression. A man who has met him cannot remain the same, says Alcibiades in *The Banquet*.[1] After him, and for long ages after, drawing their inspiration from him as from a unique source, come the Sages of the ancient world—Plato, Epicurus, Epictetus, Seneca, Marcus Aurelius, and Plotinus, to name only the greatest. It is evident from this tradition how greatly man feels the need, if he is to progress in goodness and become himself, of placing himself under someone else's direction, "so as to live," as Seneca expresses it, "in his sight, and perform all our actions as though he were watching them."[2] This school of wisdom is a transmission of life.

In Eastern tradition we find, perhaps even more firmly rooted than in the West, this need for a sage, a "guru" as the Hindus call him, a master who teaches and trains at the same time. We are confronted with a human fact: one particular way of seeking for truth creates deeper relationships between men than concerns about money or occupation.

The bonds thus created are founded in a common search for moral perfection. But among the best of men who are united in that search, there arises a feeling of relatedness which goes beyond the order of simple morality. The respect that is shown to the master has in it elements of our feelings towards the father who gave us life. Although Christianity was later to give these sentiments a new dimension, they were rooted from the first in human nature. Side by side with physical relationship, humanity has the sense of a spiritual one. The longing for a higher kind of life, for spiritual life in the most normal sense of the word, is the basis of this relationship in the natural order.

Some people do not seem to feel the need for spiritual dialogue,

[1] 215.
[2] *Letters to Lucilius*, 11, 8–9.

or find themselves incapable of it. By temperament or because of circumstances they regard it as a waste of time, or at best a kind of service that may have some beneficial effect on them, but hardly in proportion to any effort on their part. In other words, the relationship of direction can flourish only in someone who is gifted with the finest tendencies of nature.

How could it be formed in anyone in the absence of all desire? There is a certain coarse way of looking at life, a certain primitivism of thought, an avid drive for success, a lack of delicacy in contacts with others, which kills in advance all possibility of true relationships in any sphere whatever. For these to be established, there must exist a degree of community of desires and ideals, and this may as easily be absent among believers as found among unbelievers. It is not faith that is in question here, but a certain attitude to life. Some people would call direction a luxury simply because they are lacking in sensibility as regards true human values. For the need of direction to be felt, it must be founded in man's natural desire for an inward life.

On the other hand, we should not be in a hurry to suppose the mediocrity of another's being, for there are many in whom the absence of roots is only apparent. They may be unawakened, or have limited powers of expression, or be suffering from the effects of an unhappy childhood. Such cases nowadays are more and more frequent. How often do we find a man who wants to deepen his spiritual life, to be helped in its development, but who is building on sand or running up against unexpected difficulties for lack of the elementary natural foundations! Such people have never had a really affectionate relationship with their parents; they have grown at the mercy of chance meetings, or of their instincts. Or else they have been marked at an early age by a father's or a mother's authority that was crushing or possessive. They are tempted to transfer to the new relationship which is being offered them the reflexes of childhood. Or more likely still, they are meeting for the first time a relationship that is simple and true. They do not know how to find themselves in this mysterious world where there are no points of reference. How could anyone be at ease in such a state of ignorance, or suffering from the deviation of his most elementary human feelings?

If it were only those in search of direction who were affected by this absence of roots! What so often complicates the situation is that the director himself is quickly overwhelmed in the presence of such cases. He runs the risk, by his own excesses or defects, of being the involuntary author of so many catastrophies! He does not know the nature of a true relationship in this domain, because he never had the experience of one when he was young. He has bitter memories of directors who were no doubt saintly men, but who in the difficult moments of war, captivity, or trial had nothing to offer but conventional reactions and the emptiness of words prepared in advance. No human warmth came through. That absence of human feelings—or at any rate the constraint that is imposed on them—is sometimes overcompensated in others by the opposite excess. They allow their zeal to overflow in expressions of a natural tenderness that has not until now found its outlet. This is a kind of compensation for the paternity which has been denied them, or else simply an incapacity to see themselves clearly or keep themselves under control. These two sorts, with their excesses or deficiencies, are equally incapable of undertaking spiritual dialogue, because their natural affections are out of place.

For one person to be able to entrust himself to another, without fear of being engulfed or constrained, he does not need to have great intelligence or much knowledge of the world, but simply to be himself and be true. Everyone remembers those old priests like Bernanos's Curé of Torcy. They do not fit into any category, and remain always within the limits of their nature and their experience. They do not talk like a book, but they listen to you with trust, and answer you with simplicity and good sense. All the other priests of Ambricourt go to them with their problems. The roots of their being lie deep enough and their natures are consistent enough for the most unexpected admissions to produce no reaction of withdrawal in them, no panic, no misplaced tenderness. A real dialogue can be established with them because they are sure enough of themselves to impart confidence to the secret zone of your own being of which you yourself are ignorant, and which will be revealed to you little by little through the gift of their attention.

2. THE SPIRITUAL DIALOGUE AND THE NATURAL ORDER

These strong natural foundations are all the more necessary to a director as he comes into contact with individuals in whom personal integration is still far from complete. It is to this that he must first consent and apply himself, if he wants to make possible a relationship of a spiritual order. He must begin by recognizing and accepting the natural conditions of all relationship.

Only those who have never made the slightest attempt at spiritual direction will be astonished at this assertion. No effort of will can dispense an individual from allowing his natural forces, and particularly the affective ones, to develop. One who is receiving direction must feel himself to be loved before he can give his confidence. But he himself does not know what he wants, because he has probably never had very deep relations with anyone, and has never understood himself. You talk to him about the love of God. You tell him to give himself to others and to love them. But what do these words mean to him? He has never been loved. So you must love him to start with. Then he will know what you are talking about. It is only in concrete human relationships that love is learned, not in books or at lectures. A spiritual father has to know everything for his pupil, and must help him to discover what it means to exist for someone and in relation to someone. This is the beginning of a real adventure. And it is happening more and more often nowadays, because people have learned things theoretically before they have experienced them. They talk about love before they know what it is. The director can so easily go astray if he is not himself at ease in this domain, and then everything becomes confused. The spiritual relationship that his pupil expects from him in all good faith cannot be established unless the pupil himself knows what a simple human relationship should be. He must first of all be somebody's son.

There are cases then in which the director must find the resources in himself to be father and mother to the one who is coming to him. He must not be frightened, and must not refuse himself. He must realize what is happening, how much he is capable of, and what the other can bear. The affection of the natural order that he then shows, if it is real and true, is the best preparation for the spiritual relationship, the nature of which is still unknown to the seeker in spite of his desire for it. Little by little, as his trust and assurance grow, he will discover what it was that without knowing he came to seek.

These human values cannot be treated as already established, be supposed to exist, or be taken for granted. This would inevitably result in cruel disappointments. Still less should they be regarded as negligible or dangerous. They must simply be put in their place. It is a truth of the natural order, and is verified every day, that to the extent to which a boy or a girl has had the experience of a real love relationship with father and mother, they will know how to relate to a wife or a husband. Everything is experienced within the context of the human being. We approach God with the heart that our fathers and mothers have given us.

There are some perhaps who will feel it strange that these human sentiments should be evoked in relation to a reality of so high an order as the spiritual life. Insistence on this point may appear to them as an infidelity towards grace, or a concession to the spirit of the world. A certain kind of religious education has accustomed them to treating nature as dangerous or negligible. But to do that is to forget, as Henri de Tourville so beautifully expresses it, that nature is the form which the Lord first gave to his grace: "I have nothing to teach you other than what I have already put into your nature; it is through this that I have spoken to you and still speak; it is an act; I have not only spoken about it, I have taken part in it. This nature is precisely the form I wanted to give to my grace, which means my action in you."[1] Ignorance of its laws, or contempt for the stages of its growth, are the cause of adult crises, and, in a director, prevent his advice from getting through to its target.

The supernatural spirit will have every opportunity of deploying itself, not only in prudent action towards a nature under the bondage of sin, but also to inspire that unshakable confidence which must be sustained throughout the ceaseless repetitions and new beginnings that are a part of all education. A day will come

[1] *Light and Life,* New York, 1961.

when the pupil will discover with wonder the divine source of this patience. For the present, it is not a question of talking but of being. We can leave it to God to reveal himself through this action which is taking place on the natural level.

Moreover, a frank acceptance of nature will prevent us from being misled. There are some people who are virtuous as a result of education, who do not appear to have any problems. In reality, their characters are no more integrated than is the case with disturbed personalities, because although unaware of it, they are the reflection of an environment, and the integration has not been personally assumed. Opposition, trials, or contact with a new environment would quickly reveal the fragility of this apparent equilibrium. But so long as unforeseen circumstances have not produced a shock, a director unaware of the background might be imposed upon by a facile, unquestioning nature of that sort.

In all this, we have to learn to accept nature at its proper value, not to overestimate it or play tricks with it, but to make use of it. Our contact should be a source of self-knowledge for the one we are directing, teaching him to love himself as he should, and to have confidence in himself. To mortify nature— we will some day have to speak in these terms—is not to stop its expansion, to distrust its desires, to deprive it on principle of its useless comforts. As if, for example, we were to worry about the attachment that the directed feels for the director! We have to lead him on, not to cut him off. To do otherwise is to implant from the start another cause for ingratitude in the heart of someone who perhaps has too much to bear already. Rather let this being who has asked for our help be drawn into the current of love which carries us along. It is for us, when the need arises, to be supernatural, —or to be more precise, to keep our hearts open to grace and look beyond the present moment. In this dynamic affection with which the pupil is surrounded, and which finds its truth in the direction that it takes in us from the beginning, he will learn to keep things in proportion and not to make mountains out of the difficulties on his way. It is by drawing it onwards that one respects nature, not by preventing its development.

Too frequent warnings lend more importance than is necessary to their objects. They lead to the false problems that so many people invent for themselves later on, and which become such sources of useless torment for their spiritual lives. Let us begin, as we were saying above, by recognizing and accepting the normal conditions of every relationship. All our lives we must do this, so it will be as well to get used to it from the start. The affection that we feel for the person we are training, and in which natural inclinations play their necessary part, will draw into its movement the one to whom it is given. The son learns to love by the very way in which he is loved.

In this integration there is one point that the director must watch, if the embryonic relationship is not to become closed in on itself: the subject's emotional environment. The danger for a person without a background and without friends, who comes to us isolated in existence, is the danger of the only child. We soon become, as we normally must, his one environment and his only hope. Without treating him abruptly, and taking him as he is, we must try to introduce him into a whole new world of relationships. He should be concerned with others, it is sometimes suggested; he should join a movement. The thought being that he will find a sense of relationship in that way. But this is often premature. He must first discover the existence of the world of relationships for himself. Action conceived as the carrying out of orders may take a person out of himself and still, because of the devotion it requires, leave him alone. What he needs first of all is a family. He will learn what it means to love through the love that is given to him, and in which he knows himself as an object of relatedness. The relationship of the director with him becomes deeper as he begins to live in an open and cheerful environment. The exactitude of this remark could be shown by quoting the example of seminaries or places of training: direction becomes much easier wherever there is a more developed community life. Not only does it prevent the individual from turning in on himself; it creates a climate in which real relationships can be built up. So long as this totality of human relationships does not exist, there is a risk of spiritual direction remaining artificial, without roots and without points of reference. Looking no further, we can say that the thing which makes it easier in a Christian family is the fact of its members, young and old, living together all the year round and, if the atmosphere is not to become unbearable, having human contacts among themselves which are different from those of professors and students. They are a family. And the better founded it is, the better it achieves its supernatural finality. It is there more than anywhere else that spiritual direction has least chance of appearing as a world apart.

3. SPIRITUAL FATHERHOOD AND THE LIFE OF THE SPIRIT

For director and directed alike, the integration of nature and the possibility of normal human relationships are necessary by reason of the very respect that is owed to the relationship of the special order created by spiritual direction. It is because they have been confused that people have tried to discredit it, seeing in it only an unconscious compensation for sentiments that could not be

given free expression on the natural level. But spiritual fatherhood is a fact of which a Christian who believes in the life of the
Spirit must take account, as much as he does of natural paternity.

This spiritual paternity, of which the natural is no more than
an image, can be realized only to the extent that those who express it are living in the Spirit, and that it is seen by the spiritual
father as a participation in the unique paternity which is that of
God. At the origin of all relationship stands the truth of Our
Lord's saying: "Call no man your father on earth, for you have
one Father, who is in heaven" (Mt. 23, 9). Whatever the kind of
fatherhood we are considering, there is only one which is true,
that of "the Father from whom every family in heaven and on
earth is named" (Eph. 3, 14-15). The life a man gives to his
children is a life he has himself received, and to understand its
meaning we must go back to him who is its sole source, who
receives nothing from anyone and from whom all receive life.
This it is which makes the grandeur and sets the limits of all
paternity among men. Here is the father, says Claudel in his
"Magnificat," "joined to the generations of nature and ordained
for an end to which he is a stranger," united by the life that he
transmits "to the clustered roots of all his ancestors before him."
He exercises his role and his authority, but in the humility of one
who knows himself a link in the immense transmission of life;
he passes on a life that he receives. This law of humility is even
more the law of spiritual generation. In the flow of the life of the
Spirit, more real than the life of the flesh, the father knows himself to be both necessary and dependent. Life passes through and
is transmitted by him, but not a life of which he is the arbitrary
master. This life is the very life of the Spirit, received from the
Father and transmitted through Christ to the Church and to all
men.

It follows that this paternity is real to the extent that the life of the Spirit is real for the one who receives it. For the word "father" is to be understood "in a realistic and mystical sense which could not be given to it by those who have employed it outside Christianity, and which we may restore to it only as we become conscious once more of the profound theology that gave it its meaning among the Fathers."[1] Alone, the Christian revelation teaches us the reality of the divine paternity towards us. God is essentially the Father. By His Son, He communicates to us His life, which is that of the Spirit, in order that through the Spirit we may become sons in the Son, images of Him who is the perfect image of the Father. The act of creation by which we are born into that life depends on God alone. It is accomplished in baptism. Whether it is Peter who baptizes or Judas, it is always Christ who assimilates us to Himself in the Spirit, to enable us to live the life of God. Man is only an instrument in this domain. The sole relationship that is established between us by the communication of the sacrament is the relationship of brotherhood: we all become brothers by the same Spirit in the unique Body of Christ.

And yet, in the order of spiritual generation which of itself belongs only to God, and wherein man appears only as an instrument, the name of father is given among Christians to all those who in one way or another participate in the work of spiritual generation. "And who, then," asked Amphilochius of Iconium, "is your spiritual father? Assuredly, after God, the priest who baptized you." In the same sense, St. Paul, who teaches that there is only one paternity from which all paternity proceeds, claims for himself the title of father: "For though you have countless guides in Christ, you do not have many fathers. For I became your

[1] *Dictionnaire de Spiritualité*, col. 1010.

father in Christ Jesus through the Gospel" (1 Cor. 4, 15); and even that of mother (see 1 Thess. 2, 7, and esp. Gal. 4, 19). In the same way, in our own day, a bishop claims paternity over all those who work with him for the proclamation of the kingdom, or who through him receive its benefits. Further, many are the priests who prefer to the more or less honorific titles which are bestowed on them ("reverend," for example), that other, so much simpler and truer, which is addressed to them in the liturgy and in the celebration of the sacraments: father. We find ourselves here in the presence of a world of relationships which, like all realities of the spiritual world, cannot be enclosed within mathematical boundaries. We are inclined to smile when we hear declarations made to "spiritual sons" or "spiritual daughters," but we are nonetheless confronted here with a reality; it is that of the "continuous generation" of the children of God throughout the world, and it is right, in this order of the Spirit, to speak of paternity in a true sense. The condition of truth in this matter is to look for its source, not below, but above.

It must be in this perspective that we think of true paternity in connection with spiritual direction. Here is a reality of the life of the Church, through which someone who has experienced it may lead another on the spiritual path, for as long as that other is asking to be helped in his progress. To do this is to act as a father towards the children of God.

Spiritual fatherhood has as its basis an essential element of choice. I choose to place myself in dependence on the one whom I recognize as father. And this reveals the level of human maturity that direction requires for its exercise: in the spiritual order, a person becomes a son only to the extent that he chooses to be as a child in order that he may enter the kingdom. The act of free choice continues that of baptism, through which the

Christian accepts the gift of God. In a deeper sense, he is imitating the act of the Son, who does not cease to recognize His dependence on the Father.

On the other side, the father's, his fatherhood is the more real as it becomes a pure transparency for the unique Fatherhood, and knows its dependence on the one Spirit who alone guides our hearts. The father who is worthy of that name in the natural order knows himself to be dependent in the exercise of his authority on an order greater than himself, in which he is included. Even more is this true of the spiritual father. Despite the strength of his own feelings, and their strength is the greater, the higher the order in which he moves, —St. Paul compares them to those of a mother—, he knows himself, in this paternity of his, to be nothing but a reflection of, or a channel for, the unique paternity of God. For him this is a means of knowing God; the more his heart suffers or rejoices in this child-bearing, the more he sees God's working in him. It is the Father who does these works in me, said Our Lord (see Jn. 14, 10). He will not be tempted to enclose himself in the feelings he has, so as to enjoy his role or claim a privileged place. He knows the source of his authority. Here lies the deepest cause of the attraction exercised by a true spiritual father.

The Relationship in Its Beginnings

The exercise of this fatherhood-by-participation is ruled by its character of being a channel or transparency for the unique Fatherhood. That character is its strength, and at the same time sets its limits. We may see this by considering some examples:

To begin with, if we are to give someone the help God wants us to give, we must receive it from God. That is immediately evident. In practice, this means the constant exercise of true detachment, which alone opens us to love. The will that we should receive the one who comes to us as from God alone, purifies from the beginning the natural eagerness that inclines us to enter into him as into a conquered country, and make him our possession to enjoy or command. The grossest manifestations of this eagerness are not always the most dangerous; no doubt they will stop all progress in the first place, but at least they are perceptible. One of the most common faults, but less easily discerned, is that of fixing in our imagination at the outset a picture of the kind of person we think we ought to be. Sometimes it arises from fear of doing the wrong thing, and sometimes so as not to commit ourselves; but in either case it is ourselves we are looking for, and not the other. The truth is that we must imagine nothing at all, either in one direction or another. We must be like the beam of a balance, responsive to the weights that are put in the pans, and dipping this way or that as the load requires. In so doing, from the start of the relationship, we shall pass beyond the natural feelings, good and lawful though they may be. Our desire is to be under submission to grace alone, and to meet the other on the level at which God is joining us to him.

The responsiveness that brings about this counter-movement is what gives us strength. Right away, the other enters into our inner life. He is not a distraction for us, from which we shall have to shield ourselves by prayer. We carry him *in* our prayers, and the very personal concern that we feel for him is the working of the charity that God pours into our hearts. Not that we consider ourselves so very necessary to the other, or that we imagine he would be lost if we were not to answer his call: God, whose will is the salvation of all men, has plenty of other means for saving him. But it is he who from now on becomes necessary for us to approach God. He, for us, is God. For we cannot say that we love God if we are not willing to carry with Him, and with all our heart, this being who has been entrusted to us.

At these depths, and from the beginning, we shall avoid both exclusive or possessive attachment and that abstract, fearful, impersonal love which discourages so many good intentions. We love with the whole of our being, but our love is borne up by the unique love of God, and then without his realizing it, the other is drawn along in its wake. We are faced here with a work of grace in which we must collaborate. An attachment is born in us which stirs all our affective powers, but which can grow only in God. Insofar as we remain faithful in our guidance of the early stages, we shall later see with increasing wonder how God, who asks our all, can be so great a bond of love.

Reserve and prudence may have their parts in this attitude; fear has none. Respect will translate itself in practice into that willingness to stand aside which is always necessary when the creature is face to face with a divine work, whether it is being accomplished in us or in someone else. It is thanks to this that we shall avoid making an absolute of ourselves or him, and stopping short at the grace of the moment. We shall know ourselves, along with the other, in our mutual relationship, which draws us forth from God and leads us back to Him. It is the application to an individual case of that movement of the universal charity which, always personal and always open, carries forward the whole Church in the unity of Christ.

Whatever progress the other may achieve thanks to our help, this same attitude will preserve its ongoing in its first purity. Which means that we cannot engender him into the new stages where God is leading, except in as much as we respect the work of grace and allow ourselves also to be carried higher up and further on. In this progressive detachment we discover, far beyond any felt presence, the invisible ties which God binds forever about those who allow themselves to be fashioned by him. This being, who has grown under your hands, in your spirit and your heart, you will keep as a son if in that paternity at its most intimate you recognize the work of God. Fatherhood degrades itself when it no longer knows its origin, whatever the degree in which it is exercised. St. John calls the faithful "my little children," but with them, he acknowledges God as the only Father.

Just as it should be impossible for a spiritual father to enclose himself in the sentiments that he feels or arouses, in order to take pleasure in them, so must he not in this work he is undertaking be the dupe of progress achieved or results obtained. He must see himself as dependent on an action which it is not for him to rule as he wishes, for it is the work of God in the being who has been entrusted to him. Accordingly, his manner should exclude all paternalism and arbitrariness. Rather than fixing in advance a plan of life and demanding its execution, his aim should be to remove the real obstacles which prevent a person from opening himself to the light of God. Then, as happens in natural education, the director strives to release the subject's inner forces, the dynamism of his nature, as being so many indications furnished by grace. It is not that he disregards the faults, the impurities of intention, the manifestations of egoism, or the remaining traces of adolescence, but that he obstinately refuses to allow himself to be hemmed in by them. Even regarding difficult cases, he is aware, through long experience, that a spiritual life which is sufficiently turned towards God and towards other people has a therapeutic efficacy equivalent or superior to that of psychiatric treatment.

Differently from many directors who are full of good will but inexperienced in the life of the spirit, he attaches importance to details only for their over-all significance, and from the very first regards the love that is in a person as the best dynamic, capable of overcoming all obstacles. Much time can be saved by building up confidence, even if in the early stages one seems to be standing still. Each will learn, in this awakening love, to discern what is real from what is not: the fruits of the Holy Spirit from the simple effects of a happy temperament. And despite the uncertainties of the beginning of the new life, the director will soon no longer confuse that enduring peace which is a source of action, with a natural optimism which is inclined to work by fits and starts. He will discover the depths where, beneath all the surface conflicts, there is unbroken calm. Similarly, he will learn not to be misled by a too eager generosity. He will be able to profit from awkwardnesses, mistakes, faults even, in the accomplishment of his efforts to release the self and give it up to God. These things cannot be taught in a day or a month. Sometimes he will harden himself too much, and fall back bruised and powerless; at others, he will over-relax and let himself go too far. But these experiences, against the background of a growing love, will teach him gentleness and peace.

Only a love that is drawn from the wellspring of all paternity is strong enough to undertake such an education. It is not irritated at perpetually beginning again. It does not demand immediate results to satisfy the onlookers. It is undisturbed by the talk of people in a hurry, who have ready-reckoners for virtue and want everyone to go by the same road—their road— or who live in perpetual expectation of catastrophe. It is in the image of God, unhastening, letting the tares grow with the wheat so as not to weed out the good grain, waiting in patience for the right time. It is not deceived, and knows the way it must go; or lets God know it rather, and puts its trust in him. Even if there are days when it is discouraged by unexpected disappointments, it presses on with the absolute certainty which comes from God and in which it is ever renewing itself. Living in hope, it is not bound by time.

True progress is born out of conscious freedom and from a heart capable of self-giving. Until these depths have been reached, the director will not allow himself to be impressed by appearances of virtuous conformism, and for this reason he will not hesitate to spend a long time on the preliminaries of the spiritual life, years if need be. He will not lose the way if he keeps his eyes always fixed on the end to which these efforts lead: that each should be docile to the Holy Spirit, beginning from what he is. To this docility he will ceaselessly return, disposing his pupil to it from afar, by discreet and successive touches. A false move, the desire for quick or reassuring results, may gravely imperil the future, or fix someone who is afraid of making mistakes or causing displeasure, in a ready-made pattern of behavior. So the director prefers to ask very little, but aims always at accomplishment with a joyful heart. The little done today, if it is achieved in contentment, is the preparation for the total giving of tomorrow. In the absence of this orientation, he is building on sand. When it is there, he can afford to wait; his objective will be gained.

The only point which should cause anxiety to a director is a feeling that his pupil is inert or becalmed. Nothing is happening, nothing is moving. This would be the indication of a real obstacle, psychological or spiritual. Particularly if the one in question remains hard, enclosed in his egoism, indifferent to others, without desires. But as long as things are moving, he need not be afraid of mistakes, wanderings, falls. He should learn rather to make use of them: experience is the best training. If he notices after a while that each falling back is followed by an upward movement, reaching a higher point than the one from which the fall took place, he can take heart. The Holy Spirit is at work. It will be enough for him then to help with enlightenment, and much encouragement of his pupil to push untiringly ahead.

This fatherly patience is the very opposite of indifferent letting-be. There are spiritual fathers who do nothing but bless and reassure, just as there are fathers of families who let their children grow up anyhow. No good can be expected of such. Every true father knows when to use an authority that admits of no reply. There are inflexible demands that liberate, and prevent all turning back. Love is not afraid to make them, but awaits the right moment to do so. They are the more effective for being very rare, and from it being evident that they are the result, not of impotent impatience or of cold premeditation, but of the situation itself where love is in action. Far from being shaken by them, the son's trust is strengthened. He feels the sureness of the guiding hand. He learns to govern himself with strength and gentleness.

We must insist on this necessity of knowing when to make demands, but always in truth. There are times when it is permissible to expect someone else to have almost blind confidence in us, but first we have to earn the right to demand it. Because, when we act like that, we must be able to rely on the certainty that we shall remain faithful to the underlying drives of his nature, and the absolute assurance that later on, when he has understood, he will himself want to carry out the demand that we have made, on his own behalf. The thing to avoid, on the other hand, is paying too much attention to faults, or to habits that we cannot perhaps help noticing at the start. If there is overmuch insistence on these, or too frequent reminders are given, it is discouraging. Later, when the individual has found his point of equilibrium on a higher level, such matters, which seem essential only to those who look at the surface of things, will be swept along in the movement of life and righted of their own accord. For the moment, it is more important to be uncompromising in the elimination of fundamental obstacles, and to keep a sharp lookout for evasions and false successes. This is rough work, because it often requires of us the very contrary of what we were expecting; and it plunges the directed into darkness and a struggle, where he has the feeling of losing everything on which up to now his assurance has been founded. The spiritual father must uphold him now with firm confidence and kindly understanding! Certain capes once rounded, liberation appears to be final: there is no going back.

We are committed, therefore, to a real struggle in bringing someone to the docility which leads him to God. It is normal to meet with resistances, especially in subjects the worth of whose personalities has not prevented the formation of various kinds of problems. "The passivity required of the soul is not commensurate with the human plasticity of the character. As soon as there is an authentic committing of the self into the hands of God, the possibilities of evolution become immeasurable."[1] We should remember the son whom Our Lord spoke of, who first refused the service that was asked of him. When he had thought about it, he obeyed his father, whereas the compliant son who

[1] "Etudes Carmélitaines," 1949, *Trouble et Lumière,* p. 212.

said yes at once, left his father's presence and did nothing (see Mt. 21, 28–32). We act in God's way when we accept each as he is and are not stopped by any human impossibility. As soon as in reality, and not merely in words, he allows us to treat him with that "liberating brutality" which ceaselessly brings him back to the level of faith, we have to teach him not to let himself become wrapped up in vain analyses or perpetual self-questionings, but, accepting himself as he is at any moment, to pass on to God. Thus from the first steps he is learning the exercise of a life of faith that will end only with earthly life itself.

The Development of the Relationship

Until now, we have been describing the relationship in its beginnings. It calls, as we have said, on the deepest elements in man: his nature, and grace. These beginnings set their mark, and it is a lifelong mark, on director and directed alike. As it develops, however, the relationship, although governed by the same principles, undergoes a maturation process. Its tone grows simpler, meetings are less necessary, and there is a certain effacement; while the subject, who has become himself, becomes also in his turn a center of relationships and begins to fulfil his own vocation.

The detachment, which takes place at the inmost level of the being, consists in appropriating nothing to oneself of the gifts that have been made to the other. There is certainly nothing harsh about it, and it inspires no distrust of the very pure affection that the heart feels. There is something in it of the natural joy that any father experiences when he sees the son who was a part of himself taking on the stature of a man. But this joy is like those moments of wonder that we sometimes feel for the beauties

78

of nature. If we try to force the mood, its grace vanishes. The spiritual father admires and passes on. He is not concerned to interfere with the freedom that he has helped to grow, and remains discreetly silent as he watches the free working of God's grace in that other heart. At this time of his life, his model becomes John the Baptist: not one who forms disciples, but one who lets them go. He called himself the bridegroom's friend, and now the bridegroom has met the bride. He rejoices, because he came only for that hour, he who was not the light, but the witness of the light. He has certainly not been the impassive witness of a struggle in which he took no part. He was involved in the fight, and knows its forces and how much hangs upon it. But now is the hour for which he came. He had prepared himself for it long before. The Lord must increase and he, John, must diminish. He has made ready for the Lord those whom the Lord is now taking to himself, and it is time for him to be numbered among the little ones to whom the Father reveals the secrets of the kingdom. He, the greatest of the prophets, the greatest "among those born of women" (Mt. 11, 11), aspires to be no more than the least in the kingdom of heaven.

It is this supreme detachment that witnesses the truth of his mission. All that he tried to do to help those whom God entrusted to him, was only means and preparation. Now he feels no regret, no sense of frustration. If he had felt any, it would be a sign that the Lord whom he claimed to serve was not everything for him. In reality, he has lost nothing. He finds again, in the one Lord of all, the sons and daughters to whom he has given life, and in this his joy is fulfilled (see Jn. 3, 27-30).

In the measure that such a relationship is founded from its beginnings in single-minded love for the Lord of all things, it will give those who experience it access to this level of faith. It has been said that direction, as it develops, becomes useless; the person who is now an adult has no further need of it. It would be more correct to say that it divests itself of its inferior manifestations. People who have reached adulthood relate themselves in a deeper way to God. In the bond which unites him to his spiritual father, the directed finds one of the most excellent forms of his dependence towards God. Through it he glimpses the true meaning of obedience, the bond of mutual love, while on the other hand he feels himself more and more free in regard to the consultations which he can still ask of his spiritual father. "I ask only to be allowed to see you from time to time, to be able to talk freely with you, so that I can judge myself afterwards by your reactions towards me." That is the formula of a mature man. The spiritual father may leave this world, and there will be no point in looking for another. "He is dead," you will say. "Live from his spirit." He has set free living forces in you. Continue on that course and see for yourself what you have to do. In the faith, the bond that unites you is stronger than death, and helps you to find again the spirit who formed you.

The Relationship Must Be Open

In describing the evolution of the relationship, we have emphasized its essential limitation; it must be developed in an ever more complete dependence on the one Fatherhood which it reveals and to which it leads. But there is another limitation of a practical sort: we must accept the necessity of its being shared, or of having recourse to external aid. No doubt we may dream of a single and continuous training, the ideal bequeathed to us by the Desert Fathers: choose for yourself among the elders the one to whom you will entrust your soul, and remain forever afterwards among his followers. We are not told whether that ideal was often realized in practice. But we should not too quickly pass over their advice. There are so many who suffer from having been through a large number of hands! Anyone who has received the confidences of seminarists or young religious will be able to say without hesitation that a lot of them have missed continuity of direction during their formative years. "I was just beginning to get used to my director, and he to me, when I had to make a change." The complaint is frequent and justified. One of the most certain causes of instability among young religious or young priests is not having been able to confide in someone intimately and constantly at an age when they had the greatest need of doing so. When first youth has passed, it will be different. But at the beginning—and the beginning may last for a long time—changes are for the most part harmful. It may be that this is the fault of the one directed, and then we have to understand what it means. But to the extent that institutions tend to favor it, we have cause for concern. The training received through a variety of programs, or as a result of meeting many different personalities, is something quite other than training by one master or one father from whom nothing is hidden. That kind of self-opening does not happen many times in one's life.

But it is evident that a personal and continuous relationship like this can become harmful in its turn if it leads to hot-house education. A spiritual father must accept the need of having an open and shared relationship.

Just as an ordinary father would not attempt to educate his son without recourse to the external aids of school, family, society, and events, a spiritual father giving his pupils training in docility to the Holy Spirit cannot neglect the daily confrontation with reality, a sort of experiment in which the disciple learns to know himself, to handle himself, to test in practice the grace he has received from God. Only we must not lose sight of the fact that action does not of itself produce such results. Action must be constantly reviewed in personal contacts, and judged in the secret places of the heart where thoughts and decisions are formed. Without that recourse, it runs the risk of being no more than conformism or social enterprise. In reality, in spiritual education which is modelled on natural education, the two aspects are complementary. Inner training is real only in confrontation with the world, but the confrontation is profitable only in conjunction with personal contacts. The lack of a father may bring about the failure of the theoretically best arranged of educations.

There is certainly grave danger of a spiritual father imagining, because he receives confidences, that he can solve all problems, and that only he really knows the one he is directing. He may even, for fear of the other's reactions, wish to prevent him from taking risks.

He must learn above all how to listen to criticism. Naturally, he wants to think his children are darlings! Besides, knowing only too well the difficulties he is up against, he is tempted to see just the positive results, and rejoices in the smallest success. We should not reproach him for trying to reassure himself in his heavy and austere task. But, as in any other kind of work, he may easily get caught in the quicksands of progress made and mutual congratulations. It is then that the criticism from outside, in its unexpected brutality, wakes him up and produces its salutary effects. While the pupil, who has been chased back into his trenches, is seeking defense and justification at his father's side, the latter must preserve at all costs the other's trust and love, and yet not refuse to face the outside attacks. The child's tendency is always to oppose family and school. The school can do nothing unless it is upheld from within the family. The father's affection and serenity will allow the child to integrate into his personality the elements that at first he encounters as obstacles. The difficulty then becomes a means of growing, and gaining confidence.

The spiritual father is therefore far from indifferent to outside criticisms, to the results of human actions, to the confrontations met with, the tastes and repulsions stirred up by life. He must use them as means to help the one entrusted to him to know himself truly, to avoid false assurance, psychological deviations, and false virtues. It is always dangerous to shut oneself up in the little world of spiritual direction, as it is to be enclosed in the little world of the family. Gentleness and interiority will allow the assimilation of revelations which, brutally made as they are by the chance happenings of life, may either discourage or arouse reactions of defense. But the parents must not protect the child from them. There is nothing more valuable for him than to learn how to bear these conflicts in daily practice. Where others stumble, he will go on his way. Besides, the parents know how to measure demands against possibilities, will not expect everything to be achieved at once, will recognize providential indications as regards action to be taken or the right time to act.

Lacking this personal education, young people can so easily be overwhelmed by action they have undertaken too quickly and alone. Then there is surprise at their failure to achieve what their first successes seemed to promise. The cause of the trouble lies in these hasty and thoughtless beginnings. Still more serious is the fact of their going into action with a rigid, imperative, or uncompromising character that puts neither themselves nor others at ease. It is as if they were mechanically obeying orders, and had never learned to take action on the personal level.

The all-important thing here is the approach. Life acts brutally, and leaves us on our own, discouraged and impotent. It is the delicacy of paternal affection that teaches us how to absorb these unavoidable revelations. The father must not say, comfortingly, "Don't worry. It's nothing." The child must feel that the father is making the situation his own, that he is assuming as his own the fault that the child has been criticized for. "All right. What are we going to do about it?" he says. This time, the child need not try to hide himself away from reality, because he feels that he is not facing it alone. In a true education, the father takes the whole of his child's load, and then teaches him to carry it. He is with him: he says "we." An unbearable situation—in itself it cannot be unbearable, but it always seems so to the person who feels himself alone—becomes a means of growing. In this way, trust is founded on a real basis, and the personality is enabled little by little to attain its full development.

There is one kind of external help in which the role of the spiritual father is at once delicate and necessary. The case arises when the pupil needs to have psychiatric consultation.

To begin with, the director must avoid panic and recognize the usefulness of this help. It is important, if he wants to go on giving his own proper assistance, that he should "be able to discern in conduct which objectively conforms with, or is contrary to, the ideal of perfection, the neurotic motivations which give it its psychological significance."[1] It is normal for the one under direction to be unconscious of these, but it would not be normal for the director to be deceived about them.

How should he conduct himself when he feels that such a course is going to be necessary? His first reaction should be one of calm. Many of the anomalies that each one of us carries in

[1] "Etudes Carmélitaines," *Direction spirituelle et psychologie*, p. 318.

himself can be resolved by taking them in a way that is frank, open, and affectionate. Some people are terrified at the prospect of going to a psychiatrist, and the best thing is to begin with regular, sensible, and confident efforts to reassure them.

The evidence is clear: we ought to learn to do without doctors, and resolve our daily problems within the family. It would be disastrous to create an obsession about consultations over the slightest psychological difficulty. A good spiritual father should be able, and especially at the beginning, to restore matters to their proper proportions. He must do this particularly at the time of adolescence, when young people tend to get everything mixed up. They will say that they have lost their faith, simply because of intense anxiety feelings about the gravity of the questions and the search that it involves, or the difficulty of facing up to other people. We must know how to help them untangle their confusions, and so help them to grow.

But, when recourse to a psychiatrist becomes useful, the director should have a dual attitude: on one hand, respect for the domain of the specialist, and on the other, an understanding and affectionate support of his pupil so that the discoveries to come will be made in an atmosphere of confidence, and will further assure the unity of the individual.

There are some directors who mistrust psychological investigations. But at least the director could have a talk with his pupil on the lines that any father would to a child who was frightened about some necessary surgical operation: There is nothing to be afraid of. He knows his business. Do what he tells you. A psychiatrist should be able to count on the confidence and intelligent help of the priest, when he is operating in his proper domain.

But the director must not surrender his own responsibility. It is he who, like the father of a family once again, creates the atmosphere thanks to which the operation has the best chance of success. He teaches the way to bear shocks with faith, and how to draw concrete conclusions from life. In particular, in difficult cases or during prolonged treatments, he helps to maintain a true spiritual life, making its points of application felt in the very midst of the disturbances that the patient is suffering. These points are often very simple, but it is important to come back to them over and over, so as to confirm the other in committing himself to God.

The psychiatrist and the priest should each remain in his place, and should not interfere with the specialty of the other. This is the best way of keeping the patient's confidence. He will be aware of this inner harmony, and will realize that it is not just a preëstablished understanding—which would give him the impression of being cheated, or conditioned—but a true harmony, existing in itself, independently of those who are trying to bring it about. Sometimes, an exchange of views between the psychiatrist and the director may be useful, and even desirable. But, first, it must not happen without the patient's knowledge, and secondly it must remain discreet so as to guarantee the necessary independence to both parties.

It is possible for a director, especially an inexperienced one, to focus too much attention in his pupil's presence on psychological problems alone. This is the very opposite of what formerly took place, when because of ignorance about them, the two domains were sometimes separated and sometimes confused. The danger here is that perspectives may be falsified, and the idea implanted that a spiritual life is possible only when there is perfect human equilibrium. That would be to fall back into a kind of humanism, supposedly Christian, from which all personal recourse to faith would gradually be eliminated. What must happen, on the contrary, is that the emotional disturbance raised by the consultation, whether of success or discouragement, should be an opportunity for the director to show how in all circumstances one must learn to pass on to a higher level. The spiritual life must appear as basically independent of the success of the psychological treatment. In this way the responsibility will be placed where it really belongs, and the director will not appear to the directed as a would-be therapeutist. That would be a sign that his action had strayed from its object.

Whatever the kind of help we are concerned with—whether it comes from life, from trials, from commitments or from psychological investigations—the important thing, underlying the more or less competent advice that may be given, is the quality of the relationship that is established between director and directed. Let it be above all a power for life and for evolution, and may it never become shut in on itself.

It will not become shut in on itself if the spiritual father, accepting outside help for his own pupils, consents in his turn to give occasional help to others who are not his. A father is willing to help other fathers over family concerns, and a priest should never refuse any of the multiple opportunities offered by his ministry or by the contacts of everyday life. So, in the case of help given to someone in the course of a retreat, you know that you will never see him again, but try to tell him what you think, in response to the trust he has shown in you, —submitting everything, however, to the judgment of his spiritual father. You will be acting like a family friend who says to a young man in a crisis, "I'm saying this to you, but you should have the whole thing out with your father." The same thing applies to the frank answer you might give to someone who has been living with you for a while and says, "You would be doing me a service by telling me what you think of me." You have to be honest, straightforward, and then withdraw without returning to the subject. It is another way of reassuring someone to let him feel the respect that you have for his own particular relationship with the father of his choice.

In the acceptance of this network of relationships and successive acts of help, the heart becomes refined and purified. The personal relationship of director and directed becomes more intimate, more "unique" one might say, at the same time as it opens out more fully. It is self-giving, respect for others, acceptance of life, openness to grace, and discretion. It is as though the whole life of the Spirit were flowing through this special relationship, and through it spreading to one here and another there, under all kinds of circumstances. Later on, no doubt, the pupil will make plenty of discoveries, on his own or through others, which his spiritual father will not have occasioned, perhaps because he has not made them himself. What counts is not the object of the discovery, but the way in which it is taken. On this point, the father remains the center of reference, but always so as to allow the son to become open to wider horizons.

The Relationship and the Person

Those who speak of direction often emphasize the necessity for detachment. The picture they give of the director is of an impassive man whom nothing moves, because he is already living in another world and has no personal attachments. He is preserved in this way from the too real dangers of excessive attachment and always-possible deviations.

Without wishing to suggest that this way of thinking is wrong —it has some foundation in facts—we should insist on the opposite necessity for the director not only to take account of the actual conditions in each pupil, an adaptation which is required in all apostolic work, but to commit himself wholly to the relationship which he accepts. This is the primordial condition for direction to be efficacious, as it is the first condition of success in all human education.

It should not surprise us, therefore, if direction, in the measure that it creates personal relationships, sets its mark on the individual. This imprint is not the consequence of the weak personality of the directed coming up against the strong personality of the director. It is quite possible for the former to have, at least potentially, more remarkable gifts than the latter. But what is certain in any case is that this relationship, through which he begins to exist, and which opens him to freedom and love, will mark him in one way or another. It is said of a man that he resembles his father. The resemblance is not a lack of autonomy. It is rather the sign of his accession to majority, when it is recognized and accepted as such.

This law of development of every human life seems to explain the existence in the Church of a wide variety of spiritual schools. These do not so much attest the multiplicity of doctrinal syntheses which satisfy the spirit, as the presence of a variety of masters and a living tradition. Perhaps in these days we have some difficulty in understanding that aspect. We are hardly more concerned with spiritualities than with spiritual fathers. We want instead to discover the spirituality of an action, of an apostolate, of an environment. Intellectual construction is useful, but it only comes later. Plato comes after Socrates, St. Paul after Christ. Our efforts are in danger of producing a mere collection of abstract ideas if we do not first meet with a man of experience who can hand on what he lives by. Even if you know more than he does, even if you are doing work of a nature that he does not understand, it is he who frees your living forces and gives you hope. The son may be beyond his father on the intellectual or social level; he nevertheless recognizes him as the one to whom he owes everything, because he has learned from him what cannot be learned from books: a certain way of taking existence, a certain way of loving. The father always rediscovers himself in the son, even if the son does things that the father never thought of.

There is no lack of spiritualities today, but there is of masters. People regret the mistakes of their youth. Yet they were taught all the necessary ideas, and heard all about the life of grace, renunciation, the cross, faith . . . But explanations remain abstract, or give rise to all sorts of warped notions, if they are not brought to life around a man. How many read St. John of the Cross who read him too soon, or in the wrong way! They do not have the approach which, in this domain, is essential. And that is learned only at a father's side. Most of us can remember one of those masters whose teaching was felt to be poor at the time and hardly impressed us. A deficiency like that may be regrettable. And yet, years afterwards, the long-forgotten teaching has still left vivid in the memory the image of the person who gave it. He in his reality was the living corrective of the insufficiencies of the doctrine. There is a law of life in this: every spiritual notion is in danger of being wrongly understood, and in any case remains

without savor, if it does not carry the personal mark of the man
who incarnates it.

The Analogy of the Relationship

What name are we to give, among human relationships, to the
one of which we have just been describing the character and
evolution? Can we speak of a paternal relationship? In a domain
so complex, it would be unwise to try to condense all its aspects
into the unity of a single notion. Direction, as we shall see, includes the most varied kinds of help. But where it is fully
realized, perhaps there is no better way of describing it. As fatherhood does in man, it calls on the most intimate components of
our human and spiritual natures. Like fatherhood, it opens out,
in the disinterestedness of a love that asks no return, all the capacities for giving that there are in a man. And more than this,
because it is of the order of the Spirit, it requires of those whom
it binds together, the free acceptance of choice and the opening
of the heart to God.

In speaking of it we have alluded to the divine fatherhood, but
we hope no one will be mistaken about our thinking. Neither in
connection with the spiritual relationship nor in that between
father and son should we wish to open the door to some kind of
clerical paternalism. This could not in the remotest fashion
represent the fatherhood of God, with its infinite respect for the
freedom of the individual. But we may attempt to develop in relation to a particular case the immense "analogy" in which the
unique Fatherhood gives us, through its creatures, images of
itself. These images are not simply the external reproductions of a
reality that we could never attain, but a sort of participation

thanks to which finite beings, in the activities that they are called by nature or by grace to exercise, are carried along in the movement of creative love, and become the repositaries of a power that is greater than themselves. In the distinterestedness with which a spiritual father undertakes, for no advantage except for love, to commit himself to the service of another in order to help him in his way to God, there is a dynamism which, if we could perceive its source, would seem to spring from the depths of divine compassion. And for this reason the spiritual father, to the extent that he is neither afraid of allowing himself to be invaded by this force nor desirous of possessing it, feels himself to be of no account in comparison with his work. In his faithfulness he becomes a coöperator with God in the greater work of the edification of the Body of Christ. It is not his own son whom he engenders, but a child of God. This is a spiritual work, if anything is, not because it is exercised in a supra-terrestrial order, but because down to its humblest manifestations it makes a man dependent in all things on the Spirit of God.

It is the dependence of the relationship in regard to the unique reality of God which is also the source of its strength. Undoubtedly, especially at the beginning, there is a danger that transference or substitution may strain the newly established relationship. The director should be aware of this. But, beyond what he accepts as passing means which will eventually be recognized as such, he perceives and is strengthened by the quality of the relationship that unites him to those who have entrusted themselves to him in this special way. It is not an occasional relationship, like that of a doctor or a psychiatrist with a patient. That sort is paid for, and properly so. The payment is a recognition of the autonomy of persons who render one another services requested in passing. With spiritual direction we move into the order of charity, which is not paid for, which endures, and is joined in its smallest transient acts to the extraordinary love of God, and is a revelation of Christ. The relationship of direction, among others in the Church, is one of the "joints" which knits together the whole body of Christ and builds it up in love (Eph. 4, 16). Existing within a human frame, as St. Paul reminds us, it is not of the order of flesh, which is limited and passing, but of the order of Spirit which, through each individual relationship accepted for Christ, incorporates our lives into the immense tracery of love that eternally unites the sons of God.

CHAPTER THREE

The Formation of the Spiritual Director

CONFRONTED with the ideal of spiritual direction, one is tempted to ask who would dare to undertake such a responsibility. The best thing might be to nominate people for the task, rather like those old-time monks who had the youngest ones under their conduct. But basically the same question might be asked about fatherhood. How could a man dare to give life to another being, and undertake the whole of his upbringing, if God had not given him the instinct and the strength to do it?

Direction is, in fact, like the discernment of spirits, of itself a free grace, not acquired but imparted by God, independent of the merit of the one who receives it. It is, in the supernatural order of the guidance of others, what instinct is in the natural order.

An affirmation like this does not solve the practical problems. Just as there are plenty of men and women who rightly complain, in spite of the instinct with which nature has endowed them, that they were never properly prepared for marriage and bringing up children, so there are numbers of priests who, not without some justification, lament the fact that they were given no training in the exercise of the charisma that they had perhaps received.

"It is incredible," as they often say, "that we had no teaching on this subject at the seminary." But it must be admitted that many are afraid to commit themselves; the failures that we see in ourselves and others are hardly encouraging. One thing is certain: priests frequently own up to their incompetence in this domain. "We are not specialists" is the excuse that most of them give.

Certainly, the charisma has to be there, like the instinct. Without that, nothing can be done. But often a priest is thrown into action without having had time to turn round. And then, to be prepared at least to exercise the gift that everyone has in him to a greater or lesser degree, would allow the individual to apply himself to it more correctly when the time came. And lastly, apart from the charisma, is there not an obligation on every priest to acquire to some extent the habit of direction, just as discernment may be acquired, by means of books, study, and other people's advice?

It is here that we come to the question of the director's training.

What priests would really like is a book; a manual, as one of them said, that could be read for years, and would give a few principles that could be constantly referred to, whatever the ages, the situations, and the mentalities of those seeking help. Others are convinced that there must be a procedure applicable to the majority of cases. Something, perhaps, in the nature of a technique?

All the awkward expressions of these sad complaints at least show that training is not easy. It involves, as we shall see, the putting to work of the whole man in his integrality. There is no discipline in which it is more necessary to be committed with all that one is, and in which the balance between the various orders must be more carefully preserved. Because, after all, the principles are simple enough, and a hasty reader might be tempted to think it would be equally simple to put them into operation. An inexperienced person might even regard them as simplistic, a little like the bits of advice that a producer or a conductor might jot down on paper to help his stand-in or the performers. It is true that one could say: Have a few firm principles, a minimum of personal experience, some good advisors, and, if you are given the responsibility, throw yourself boldly into the water. But anyone who thought these suggestions were sufficient would be far from the mark. In practice, things are more delicate.

Above all, we have to arrive at a right mixture between the various elements that contribute to a director's formation. Intellectual study is not enough: the most learned man in the world may be a wretched teacher. Receptiveness to others and a practical knowledge of human nature are necessary to the art of dialogue, but if we limit ourselves to these, they keep us on the natural level. A director is concerned with them only to guide the directed towards a greater docility to the action of the Holy Spirit.

The over-all aim, then, is the formation of a man who is learned, experienced, and religious, never losing sight of the fact that it is the assumption of each of these elements by the higher one that makes a good director.

1. KNOWLEDGE OF THE SPIRITUAL LIFE

St. John of the Cross and St. Teresa both insist on the necessity for knowledge, and speak in harsh terms of the grossness of directors whose ignorance of the ways of God is equalled only by their pretensions to teach everything. "Such people do not know what spirit is," wrote St. John of the Cross. "It is a great insult that they are offering to God with their contempt, putting their coarse hands where God puts his." St. John of the Cross says that they are a major obstacle to spiritual progress, worse than the devil, worse than the mind itself. Scores of examples could be quoted of well-intentioned directors whose ignorance, sometimes mistaken by themselves or their admirers for evangelical simplicity, leads their followers into the quicksands, or even into the more terrible experiences of illusion and neurosis. A true director must never cease to educate himself. Ignorance is no excuse. Also to be dismissed are those who claim that a little psychology and common sense are enough, or much love of God. It is contempt of the divine order if man does not use his natural powers to do what they are supposed to do.

Having stated that a director must possess a wide range of theological, psychological, and spiritual knowledge, we must at once explain the way in which he should possess it; for it is the way of knowing rather than the possession of knowledge that enables one to help others. No doubt he must read the spiritual authors, but not in the same way as someone who is making an exhaustive study in view of a thesis on a writer, or a history of spirituality. What he is seeking is a culture that will be both revelation and stimulation. His object is to discover, through the whole history of the Church and from his reading of Scripture, the constant and yet infinitely varied ways in which God draws men to himself. Above all, it will be useful to him to have read a few of the greatest authors, to be able to refer to their most important passages, comparing them and coming back to them again and again.

Alongside the most modern spiritual writers, and the periodicals which endeavor to meet the needs of contemporary spirituality, the great authors of the Christian tradition must also be read, especially those of the earliest times. It is regrettable that so few priests during their training should be inclined towards the "Christian sources" of our faith and our spiritual life. They read only the cold summaries of the works in histories of spirituality. How much they would gain from reading some actual books of St. Augustine or St. Bernard, to say nothing of the great Eastern sources from which the best of Christian spirituality has been drawn!

In those early times, spiritual literature took the form of apothegms, terse formulas in which a whole experience is condensed: those of the Desert Fathers, the *Centuries* of Maximus the Confessor, or the hundred *Capita Gnostica* of Diadochus of Photike on the means of attaining spiritual perfection. St. John of the Cross was to give similar shape to his "Discourses of Light and Love," and St. Ignatius to his "Rules for the Discernment of Spirits." Their pithy expression is an invitation to constant reading and re-reading, so as to build that solid basis the judgment needs in order to understand the cases that present themselves. They echo the manner of the Books of Wisdom or the Gospel parables: it is not for abundance of knowledge that they are sought, but for their inward penetration and spiritual savor. Their aim is not to help us know, but to help us live.

Should we give pride of place to the specifically mystical authors like St. Teresa of Avila for example, or St. John of the Cross, or Marie of the Incarnation? Many seem to find them too lofty, and their language too out-of-date. But whatever graces of God we may be called to receive or to witness, it can never be fruitless to admire its wonders. The heart is refined by them, and learns to envision the end to which the life of the Spirit leads. Naturally, there is a danger of their being misunderstood if they are read without a guide, without initiation, or prematurely. We need not dwell on the absurdity of reading them out of snobbishness, or trying to find in oneself the states they describe, but still we must be on our guard against the discouragement and the mistakes into which we may fall as a result of unsuitable methods of study. How many have found the writings of St. John of the Cross a stumbling block because they had not had the aid of, or recourse to, any worth-while introduction to his thought. Had they done so, they might have discovered in his invitation to Nothingness and to the austere Ascent a doctrine of liberation, and one which surrounded them, from their very first steps, with love. The same could be said of the study of the great spiritual writers of the seventeenth century, Lallemant, for instance. These are for adult readers, and their insistence on the purification of the heart may lead to a calamitous self-analysis among some who are far from having attained the robust strength of the men of those days. Reading them is a source of danger if it becomes an excuse for ignoring the foundations. It really requires the help of a director.

A frequent danger attending the choice of these books is that they may be judged ill-adapted to, or out of touch with, the needs of our time. The spirituality of an earlier period seems remote and disembodied. To yield unreflectively to this criticism would be to misunderstand the most fundamental laws of any training. There is no question of transporting into our century the ways of acting and speaking of former times. But the people who can give the answers to the spiritual problems of today are just those who can stand back sufficiently far from the present to grasp the essentials and, in the midst of its preoccupations, remain aware of their transitoriness. If the nineteenth-century writers so often seem to us old-fashioned, is it not because of their lack of culture? The Revolution had decapitated the great monastic families, and the necessity of pushing ahead as quickly as possible frequently led our fathers into that romantic style which we find repugnant. We shall undoubtedly fall into the same rapid obsolescence if we are not careful to incorporate ourselves into a living tradition. It is precisely because of his culture that a Newman, in this domain as in others, does not disappoint our expectations.

Incorporation presupposes a family. Spirituality is not engendered by the haphazard reading of thick volumes during one's time at the seminary. That is a frequent mistake among young clerics, and chiefly among those who are aware of their deficiencies in this respect: they look for it in libraries. The great spiritualities have been born in community, and have been *lived* by men before they were expressed in words. One of the reasons for the success of Father Voillaume's books is that while they reëxpress the most traditional points of view, they are also the fruit of a communal experience of living.[1] Here is the source of the radiance of all the great spiritual epochs. From that point of view, a communal life founded on the utmost regard for a total consecration to God is the finest initiation into a true and safe knowledge of the spiritual writers. Three months of novitiate and a little experience is worth all the lecture courses, or rather, the former alone will allow us to profit from them. To train directors, it is not enough to send them to courses on spirituality or to set them to write theses on the questions. What will be the use of the teaching or the work, if it has no foundation in

[1] The same observation could be made of the works published by members of the community of Taizé. Their success is above all due to the fact that they are the reflection of an experience gained in community. See, for example, Roger Schutz's *Unity: Man's Tomorrow,* London and New York, 1962.

experience? And that can be gained only in life, in a tradition and in a community. In this sphere more than in any other, knowledge must remain on a level with life. Without that bond, the results are sometimes grotesque; and particularly saddening because of the misunderstandings to which the confusion leads.

Characteristic of our time is the lack of writers in whom a spiritual life is united to the life of the Church in her sacraments and her apostolic functions, and who do not separate piety and doctrine. For this reason, the older writers are often more precious for us than the moderns. They remain close to the Scriptures, and in their commentaries on them express the purest spiritual teachings. Their way of seeing things helps us to create the unity we need. On this point again, Newman is a model for the reading of the early Fathers. But even with the best authors, there is a risk of remaining more on the level of intelligence than that of the heart. The ideal would be a spiritual commentary on Scripture, like those made in the past by the Eastern and Western Fathers, which would help us to impregnate with the riches of the Scriptures our lives, our actions and our prayers.

Among the kinds of knowledge which are necessary today for a future director, psychology seems to take precedence over the others. We have already spoken in the second chapter of the invaluable help it affords in the exercise of fatherhood. And it is thanks to psychology that directors can proceed less empirically than they used to do. We have become conscious of the proper spheres in which psychology and direction should be exercised in turn. It would be unpardonable for us not to have a minimum of initiation into these matters. There are plenty of books nowadays which enable us to learn the essentials without becoming specialists, and particularly about the connections between psychology and the spiritual.[1] A minimum of acquired knowledge will limit the damage that can be done by those who have no flair, and will allow those who have to employ it with more certainty. Even more valuable perhaps than reading, when circumstances make it possible, is a fairly extensive conversation with a psychologist who is treating someone we are ourselves concerned with. Conversations like this will often encourage us to continue along a difficult road, when we feel that agreement has been established between the psychologist and ourselves, even though the means of investigation cannot be the same on either side.

But we must beware of enclosing ourselves in these studies. The director must be in closest touch with everything that concerns a man, the environment in which he lives, and all the rest. But his technique is elsewhere. It is not as a psychiatrist that he approaches those who seek his help, but as a spiritual director. There is a very real danger nowadays of becoming attached simply to the psychological point of view, and there was more than a sly thrust behind the remark of a priest who came back from a conference on direction and said that everything was discussed there except spiritual direction. The opposite excess to those of ignorance, empiricism, or distrust is not seldom that which lies in wait for young priests who are happy to find in the study of psychology the revelation of, and perhaps liberation from, their own complexes. Relying on quickly acquired knowledge, they are too easily apt to put other people into categories. The same tendency is found even among psycho-therapists. Or else they will dismiss as worn out or old-fashioned the traditional

[1] One that we particularly recommend is G. Cruchon, S.J., *Dynamic Psychology*, London and New York, 1965.

advice that they may perhaps have never completely understood, and then, strong in their acquired psychology, imagine that one has to wait for someone to come into balance before he can be awakened or go on growing in the spiritual life. In this they ignore how a real spiritual life can unify an individual from above, or at least help him to accept himself.

Mention should also be made of the value, when they are possible, of exchanges between directors. Naturally, there may be sessions for general training, set up for a particular group of priests, or open to all without distinction. But being addressed to a large number, they must necessarily remain on a theoretical and general level. Probably there should not be too many of them. Much more useful are exchanges in small groups, either for priests of the same age, or for those with the same functions, where each member can bring up the difficulties he has met with, or else there is a group discussion of one selected case.[1]

Regarding our quest of spiritual and psychological knowledge, we must never lose sight of the fact that the best educators are not necessarily those who have studied for the longest time. It is, of course, always to our advantage (and therefore to the benefit of those whom we direct) if we persist in our reading and study and meditation, but on the other hand we must take care to keep our knowledge on the level of life. A not uncommon temptation facing the newly "erudite" counsellor is to seek out all the various subtleties of a case before him, rather than give the judgment or advice (imperfect though it may be) which is so earnestly sought of him. The neophyte spiritual director especially must keep in mind that much of his pastoral art will come

[1] One might consult in this regard André Godin's *The Pastor as Counselor* (New York, 1965), and Raymond Hostie's *The Discernment of Vocations* (New York, 1963).

to him only through experience, and this is what we mean when we say that knowledge must keep on a level with life. It is for this reason, therefore, that we now pass on to our second question, which concerns experience and openness to others. For all our pastoral training and learning is directed to only one thing, and that is practical application.

2. OPENNESS TO OTHERS

It is all a question here of keeping a balance. Equally incapable of undertaking spiritual direction are those who have never studied or have given up studying, and those who shut themselves up in their books, feeling that they can never be ready to face the world of men.

Let us admit that to begin with a balance between the two is difficult. The young are always a little bookish and full of theory. For them, knowledge is an attempt to supplement their lack of experience. Here, the older ones have the advantage, and if they remain open to the stimulation of younger spirits, they will renew their own as well. But it is disappointing for the young to come to realize, when they have already learned so much, that there is still everything to learn. How could it be otherwise? The important thing is not to be deceived, and to be aware of one's age. As life goes on, it is knowledge that in its turn becomes difficult to acquire. There is not enough time to read everything. The individual is so soon outstripped by the progress of knowledge. It is the same for the spiritual director as it is for the doctor. His dexterity in practice compensates for his being quickly left behind in the realm of theory.

The critical moment comes when the young director must leave his books for mankind. How deeply one could wish for this passage not to be a rupture! That is often, alas, what happens. The too sudden plunge among men brings him to discredit the teaching he has received. "All my studies were quite useless to me," he says. Judged like that, there is a chance that they will prove to have been badly done, and one might anticipate that the contact with men will be no better. The point of view of the man of experience cannot be that of the student, but there should not be a hiatus. To avoid it, no doubt, a certain way of looking at studies and experience is necessary. But it is still more valuable that the contact between generations should be maintained in mutual esteem. The young can learn so much from an older man, who is refreshed in his turn by the stimulus of new blood. There is no question, then, of abandoning what one has learned, but there must be balance. Little by little, life indicates proportion. Experience affords short cuts to a quicker understanding of what to others may seem pure theory.

One means of securing this passage while maintaining unity is to make full notes of experiences as they come. This is a habit that should be formed early, writing down what is remembered of chance contacts, visits, happenings, words heard, personal reactions. Even if they are not re-read, these notes are a means of training the attention. They accustom us to objectiveness, which is so necessary and so difficult in relation to others. To begin with, we are awkward and constrained in attempting to write, wondering what use it is. But once we have the trick of it, it records for us that unique flavor which is found in meeting with another individuality. No gap is felt between theory and practice; but practice to which reflection is daily applied, helps us to understand the theory. If it is to be fruitful, this habit of writing obviously requires that we should seize on the uniqueness of each individual, and not treat him as "psychological material," just another case to fill up a file. There is much to be gained from the opinions of a wise colleague; it is good to have someone read the observations we have made and to see his reactions. This is a further means for developing those fundamental qualities of the true director: attention, and the capacity for reflection on experience.

Experience is acquired as a result of conversations. It is vitally necessary that the director should learn the art of dialogue and human relationships. He should do it, moreover, in a particular spirit. He is setting natural qualities to work which are different from those that make the leader or the man of action, the man responsible for taking decisions, imparting the necessary drive, inventing, asserting himself. These are the qualities of the teacher, no doubt, and they are not the same as those of the knower or the seeker, who comes into contact with others for a special purpose—not to act, or to give them orders, but to help them to see clearly and take decisions for themselves. We must therefore talk about the art of dialogue in the intercourse of spiritual direction.

Is it really possible to learn the art of asking questions, of getting someone to talk about the causes of his troubles, of which he is usually the last person to be aware, the art of breaking down the barriers, of helping to uncover the false motives that underlie his apparently most generous actions, and of discovering on the other hand the real inclinations of his being and the movements of the Holy Spirit? It may seem laughable to lay down principles in this matter, but the laughter could only come from those who have never tried to do it. All this used once to enter into the general art of helping souls. It is essentially a practical art, and it is difficult to give absolute rules for it and put them down in logical order. There are, however, some fundamental points in the technique which may serve to guide us.

In the first place, there is the art of the beginning. Sometimes everything hangs on those initial moments, and it is imperative that we should employ all our gifts of welcome. There is a psychological hygiene that the director must practice on himself so that his reception is relaxed, good-humored and leisurely. There are some people who receive you on the run between two engagements: "I have five minutes. What's your problem?" The interview is doomed in advance. The visitor, especially at those early meetings, should find a quiet office and an unhurried person, who makes him feel that we have nothing to do but listen to him. Very soon we shall be at the heart of the matter. It is not possible to have a large number of interviews and still keep this attitude; time is limited, and we have to think about the next job. This is what makes direction so difficult for teachers, people with administrative responsibilities, writers and researchers. They are thinking about something else.

There is also the art of silence, and of silences. It requires from those who practice it much interior stillness and detachment from the self. First, you must let the other talk, so as to give him confidence. Even if you learn nothing, it will give you time to think. Above all, do not try to have an answer for everything. Your visitor does not want that. Let him begin to trust you. Allow him, if necessary, to unload on you his diffused aggressiveness against the Church, against priests, against direction. He is, in fact, trying you out to see what he can expect from you. There may be things in his attacks which make difficulties for you; do not answer them. Often these points have no importance. If you take him up on them, the conversation will get bogged down in an argument or will become impersonal. Far better to go beyond the rationalizations and objections, and help him to discover the question which he is really asking himself, often without knowing it, and which will set him free.

Silence will put you in a position to register the emotional charge of the expressions your visitor employs. Every conversation, even the seemingly most ethereal, develops an emotional resonance. This is especially true of a religious discussion, in which the finest part of the person is engaged. You must know how to listen to his story without being disturbed by it, even if it is not perfectly clear to begin with. Accept everything that comes in silence, with a smile that is relaxed and yet full of respect. At the right moment you will be ready to say the word of enlightenment and deliverance, and say it above all easily, and in such a manner that he will not be embarrassed by it. If it is not conventional, but sincere; if it does not smell of moral exhortation, even though it may be rough and incisive, it will relieve, and afterwards make everything easier.

How discreet it must be, that welcoming smile for the first confidences, if it is not to give the impression of thoughtlessness or contempt. Afterwards, when confidence is established, it will be useful to suggest the relativity of details, without need for further emphasis. But at the start, if it is not sensitively controlled, the speaker may be given the feeling that we are taking the things he says to us lightly. In this sense, one could as aptly speak of the quiet silence of the eyes as of that of the lips.

That sort of silence, which could be described also as concentrated attention to another, will allow us to go straight to the positive things he has hidden inside him. "In this sea of troubles you have been telling me about, in all these downfalls and bitter disappointments, in this double life you are leading, you feel most unhappy; you want to be yourself, to be clear before

God and man. You have fallen back time and time again into your old ways, and yet this aspiration has never until now come from your heart. That is the best part of you, isn't it? . . ." If you are able to say something like this at the right moment, confidence is established. The only possible answer is yes. The other may perhaps be too upset to say anything, but the chances are that even if he remains for years without seeing you, he will come back to you in times of difficulty. Without humiliating him in the slightest, you have touched the center of his being.

It requires great self-assurance to keep silent. Mostly, we are overly concerned to answer difficulties or correct false ideas. And so many allow themselves to be preoccupied with the impression the speaker is forming of them. God knows what sort of idea most people have of a priest when they are meeting him for the first time. Or again—and this point is so important that we shall return to it shortly—our emotions interfere with the spontaneous judgment that we form of the person who is approaching us, and prevent us from seeing him without prejudice. Occasionally, a dialogue with someone else will arouse such reactions in us that the fear of being swept away by our feelings throws us into a defensive attitude; while in some cases of youth or imprudence, the emotions aroused by a confession may be such that a relationship begun on a spiritual level will be carried very far from its point of departure. In these situations, our haste or anxiety prevent us from reaching the other person's best self. He may profit from discussions with us, but the essential thing will not have been achieved. Too many, even after years of frequentation, confess that they have never been able to talk easily to their directors. He monopolizes the conversation, they say, and tells his reminiscences . . .

A silence of the real kind is never passivity. Without wishing

PREPARING FOR SPIRITUAL DIRECTION

to give the formula any appearance of having a tactical object, which would be odious, we might say that we are going in through other people's doors so that they may come out through ours. Or better, we willingly go a long way with them so that they may come to see for themselves what they were unconsciously looking for. In fact, the difficulty is not that of knowing theoretically what should be said, but of restraining ourselves from offering brilliant explanations or giving authoritative advice, and helping the other instead to discover what he needs and getting him to admit it. This is the Socratic method, and it is appropriate to this sort of conversation, in which those who come to see us know only very vaguely what it is they want and are unaware that they are counting on us to reveal it to them.

Without being too obvious about it, we must quickly be able to clear the ground and get down to the essential questions. In one sense, there is no time to lose; others are waiting. The director must practice, always with profound respect, the art of judging men, seeing what can be expected of them and what they need. It is the art of disentangling a situation. Sharing experiences can help to train one in this art. Insight is useful too. There are some people to whom it is a grave disservice to prolong a conversation. What they are saying to you is just social chatter. You do not want to discuss politics or literature, or if that does happen it should be without illusions and without losing sight of your object. So many people imagine they have a director because they spend time with him! There is no silence on either side; only an exchange of pleasant talk. Neither is engaged in the dialogue. Just as we must know when to give countless hours and days, even at the risk of arousing jealousy in others, because we are certain of our destination and the person we are dealing with, we must equally know when to sever a relationship which is bringing neither peace nor enlightenment. During the development of a relationship we must frequently ask ourselves where it is leading. Sometimes it requires the art of short cuts, and at others, when the path has been found, we must be generous with our time. In either case, only interior necessity can guide us, and to feel it, silence is needed once again: the silence of the heart. So guided, our lips will shape the reflection or the question that breaks the ice or marks the definite advance after which there is no returning. There are words which are actions. Once said, they cannot be taken back. They must be born under the pressure of interior exigence. In general, especially at the start, we talk too much. Experience teaches us to keep quiet.

To make progress in this way, a method is desirable, and there is certainly one which will afford some short cuts. But it should not be regarded as a simple method, such as can be applied by consulting a memorandum and then not thinking about it any more for the rest of the interview. It can come only with time, demands serious exercise, and must spring from the best in ourselves. Out of these elements we may be able to draw up for ourselves something like a schema of questions which will prime a conversation,[1] and allow us to go straight to the point. This is particularly useful in the matter of discovering vocations.

But, even with such safeguards, there is a danger of becoming a slave to one's technique. One turns into a man of experience. And experience must be sensed by the other as little as possible, if only to give him confidence. If it is too sure of itself, or makes itself obvious, it fosters distrust and makes the person consulting us feel that he is immediately going to be classified as a case and will be unable to explain himself. In a conversation, while keeping track of our ideas we must be free to come and go. And

[1] See Chapter Five, pp. 172 ff.

incidentally that is why it is so difficult for this kind of exchange to take place in the confessional. There, time is short and others are waiting.[1]

More than any other, this art requires us to be completely ourselves, and not to be afraid of showing ourselves just as we are. Too much calculation, too much reserve, prevent the person who has come to us from launching out. A director must be utterly free within himself, particularly in regard to sexual problems. As Dr. Nodet has observed, "The frank and open attitude of those in charge of souls requires that they themselves should be completely at ease in regard to these problems. Their habitual and personal reserve when they are faced with sexual problems must be of a purely moral order, and must have nothing to do with unconscious fears."[2] In conversations of this sort, the only thing to do is to give oneself. One must engage in them without defenses, without preconceived ideas, and without expecting to know in advance how they will turn out. A situation can be understood only if you go into it as though it were unique and new. That presupposes a great freedom—the freedom of being able to say what you think at the right moment, and to say it in clear terms. That conduct in its turn will give the other his freedom.

There is one danger in the relationship of which every director should be aware: its artificial character. Without realizing it, everyone who comes to us for an exchange of this sort assumes

[1] This is notably the case within certain congregations of women religious, where the priest receives only in the confessional and cannot obtain an interview in the parlor. Without wishing to criticize customs which in some cases have their justification, on the other hand we can certainly say that there are occasions when this situation has grave inconveniences.

[2] "Etudes Carmélitaines," *Direction spirituelle et psychologie*, p. 324.

a character, and falsifies from the beginning the picture which he gives of himself.

A great many directors have no conception of how much their insight is affected by this fact. They believe, because they are receiving someone's confidences, that they are the ones who know him best. In fact, if they are restricted to so-called spiritual conversation alone, they are the ones who know him least. And if they are not careful to maintain their contacts with everyday reality, they run the risk of encouraging in those they direct the optical illusion of the "pure spiritual," than which there is nothing more false.

One could almost wish that a director had dirtied his hands at a job before undertaking his charge. There is always the danger, especially if he starts young, and after a long period of preparation, of falling into a spirituality that is separated, arrogant, and unreal, ignorant of the humble human condition. Or, devoting his time to souls that he thinks of as superior, he misses the profound enrichment that is given by contact with the earth. It is good to live with all comers and to be open to all things. No doubt one would be equally reserved about a director who confined himself to the reading of spiritual books and felt he was wasting his time if he gave it to the things which compose the daily preoccupations of mankind. Nor, on the other hand, should he go out of condescending goodwill to see some boring spectacle that he has no taste for; it is important that he should keep alive that human part which makes him a man among men.

Given the artificial character of the conversation of direction, we must know how to observe the one directed, at the moments when he is not watching himself. The ideal thing would be to see him as he behaves in everyday life. In any case, the director should not regard as useless the conversations that he has with him about his family, his tastes, his education, his work, or his friends, and he should not be indifferent to the tone of his voice or the way in which he speaks. The slightest gesture is revealing. It should be given our full attention. This is the human foundation that is necessary to all direction. It would be advantageous for directors to receive outside information. In a college, the observations made by superintendents, friends, or teachers are immensely valuable. Too often, directors remain ignorant of the human substratum without which a spiritual life cannot be balanced. They conceive the latter as a separate domain, and do not teach an adolescent to assume his humanity in order to become capable of an adult faith. Nor are they any more concerned to know the real face of the directed, the one he wears in his ordinary life, in the eyes of those closest to him—particularly the one he shows at home.

We spoke above of the need to know how to turn aside, politely, relationships which would be restricted to the level of a kind of spiritual worldliness. We should be wasting our time in them, even if we were spending it with people who were happily reassuring their consciences because they were talking to a priest.[1] It should be said with the same certainty that we must be willing

[1] There are some spiritual clients who make an art of wasting the priest's time. Without a doubt these people help to bring discredit on direction. They seem to be more anxious to find in spiritual conversations a confirmation of their own ideas or those of their environment than to allow themselves to be challenged. This failing manifests itself especially in a time of transition such as ours. The priest's visit provides a perfect opportunity for them to bemoan the dangers the Church is running into, or to justify themselves by giving all the reasons they have for not adapting. A priest who refuses to play this game is at once classed among those who do not understand, or among "the radicals."

to sacrifice our most valuable time to the long preparations that enable a person who does not know himself to discover and to give himself. Much patience is necessary to follow an individual's twists and turns so that he may be helped to stand in the light when the time has come. We must never grow tired of observing his reactions in these repeated trials and renewals, and of helping him through them to take cognizance of his strengths and weaknesses, and also of the action of grace in him.

As every educator must, we have often to mingle gentleness and patience with inexorability, for the direction of conscience is not simply our coming to acquire knowledge about the one directed, his problems and needs. It is a contact, a dialogue, sometimes even "open combat." It is above all an interpersonal action. The one directed, feeling that he is being hunted out of his secret lairs, sometimes develops unbelievable defenses against his attacker. The subtlest of these defenses are those which are camouflaged with generous intentions. The director must show himself in dialogue to be gently inflexible. He must put into practice what spiritual writers have at all times recommended: fighting against illusions, those devourers that proliferate as soon as one's back is turned. Let him wait as long as he has to! But let him face the other with the ineluctable requirement that in every decision he shall be sure of the purity of his motives. He must be able to say no, or simply to smile when the other tries to escape down by-paths. A little lucidity and strictness will avoid many mistakes for the future, and there will be a present refusal to qualify as tribulations what are often merely the reactions of wounded sensibility. Moreover, he must not be afraid of crises, seeing them as opportunities for growth, and must avoid the short cut of giving orders. Simply and unwearyingly he must repeat the same explanations, must show the way, must quote again and again Christ's words to Peter: You will understand one day.

Neither inexorability nor gentleness must be reactions of an authoritarian temperament or of a too easy-going nature. The director must know himself well enough not to be demanding because he is irritated, or yielding because he is weak. The other must be able to feel in us, beyond any manifestations of temperament, the will that keeps on coming back to essentials and closes the way to every attempt at flight. He must know with us that there is an act of salvation to be accomplished for everyone, and that we are uncompromisingly seeking with him to discover it and to will it, and having seen and willed it, to accomplish it trustfully. This is truly an education in spiritual discernment on both sides. All the rest is useless subtleties.

Remain truthful above all. Whatever it costs, the other must not be able to accuse us later of having misled him with lenient words. Truth alone makes free. Do not be afraid that demands which are faithful to truth will ever appear as oppression.

But in this concern for truth we must know how to restrain ourselves from eagerness to say everything at once. There is a science of the revelation of truth that must be practiced with another. Such a promise as "I will always tell you exactly what I think" betrays much inexperience. "The burden would be too great for you now," said Our Lord to His disciples. He waited for the Spirit's hour to insinuate into their hearts what would have been unbearable at first. Even so, the revelation of the Cross as He made it to them was a burden heavy enough to bear. The director must do the same: wait for the time when a revelation would be profitable. There are cases when we have to ask others to rely on our good faith. And we must also know how to protect the other against himself when he demands to be told everything. It would be just as undesirable to allow oneself to be impressed by the things he says. Wait until you can see quite clearly what it is all about, and even if you think it is serious, do not show it too quickly. How many directors have involved their pupils in impossible struggles because they were as fascinated as the latter by the difficulties they heard confessed! They ought calmly to have discovered the source of the trouble, and have kept a sense of proportion throughout. This is particularly relevant in the domain of chastity.

Since direction brings into play all the psychological powers and all the human experience that a director has, it exposes him to the great and subtle danger of psychologizing—taking pleasure in his lucidity and his analyses. Direction was formerly accused of being nothing but complacency about one's inner states; to-day, thanks to the development of psychological knowledge, it is being confused with psychotherapy. The director does indeed often find himself being pulled in two directions: the one would keep him within the orbit of psychism, and the other opens him to the spiritual world. It is certain that a moment will come when he must choose between them. As Father Godin says, "He is not there to stabilize a person-to-person relationship between himself and the pupil, either from the psychological or moral point of view, but to bring the pupil into progressively closer contact and more intimate relationship with Christ, who seeks, anticipates, and sustains his love, his thought, and his action. The golden rule of the therapist then should be: teach your patient to drop his mask and become himself. But the golden rule of the priest, the spiritual counsellor, should be the very same that

St. John the Baptist gave himself: 'He must grow greater and I must grow less'."[1]

The therapist or the psychologist try to restore a person to his normal state; the spiritual director looks beyond the present state, which he knows and accepts under its eternal aspect. Access to this order introduces into his training a third necessary element: the quality of his own spiritual experience.

3. SPIRITUAL EXPERIENCE

Real people are not mistaken about this. In spite of their personal competence and the esteem they have for human values, they seek beyond the wise man for the saint who in a personal way, like Moses, is spoken with by God "face to face, as a man speaks to his friend" (Ex. 33, 11). They draw from this familiarity both the savor and the strength that give their simplest words a force of penetration which the best-prepared speeches and the most judicious counsels lack. These words dispose a person to let himself be loved by God, which is far more important than the strict remembrance of observances, or discussions about accommodating them to the weaknesses of men. Their words have acquired in personal prayer the force of penetration of the words of God. This does not come at will, and when it does it is the most important thing that can happen.

But this experience of God must, if one can so express it, have the mark of an individual style in order to be transmitted to others through spiritual direction. It is these personal traits of the director's spiritual life that we shall attempt to describe here.

[1] *The Pastor as Counselor.*

Docility in the Holy Spirit

The submission to the Spirit that the director inculcates in his pupils, as though he himself wished to disappear from before the one Master who speaks to the heart—that submission must exist in the first place in his inner life. It must be his own mark.

Among the points at which it is exercised, there is one more important than the rest: his way of taking his charge. None must assume it of himself, even if he recognizes an aptitude for it in himself or manifests an inclination. He takes it on his shoulders only if he has received the call from God; in practice, if he is summoned to it by obedience. No good can be expected of a man who believes he was made for the direction of others, and who enters this domain as into a conquered country. The superior of a congregation whom we were questioning about the selection of spiritual directors answered without hesitation, "Those who are most anxious to be trained for the work are often the very ones who must be dissuaded." We are not far from sharing his opinion. An anxious desire to undertake direction and to be prepared for this ministry often conceals what psychoanalysts call compensatory mechanisms. It is noticeable besides that those who too readily judge themselves apt for the ministry are lacking in suppleness with others, and want everyone else to pass along the same road, their road, instead of following the astonishing variety of the Holy Spirit's paths.

So it is that the director who makes himself docile to the Holy Spirit is a simple man. He has nothing of the visionary who is consulted by others and who proclaims oracles. He is just the opposite. He does not believe himself to have, and does not give himself a mission. To those who love sensations and imposing attitudes he may appear too simple, just anybody, with flashes of humor and an occasionally disconcerting skepticism. You might say that he was trying to give the impression of not believing in it very much. He knows so strongly from experience that it is the Spirit who is at work in him as in everyone, and that the advice he gives does not make him any holier. If he knows when to be firm, his strength is not crushing, because it is so clearly felt to come from above him. It is by this dependence that it imposes respect.

Living in dependence on God, he is not anxious. He leaves to bad preachers their fluent passages about grace which comes once and once only. He does not try to frighten anyone, but to face him with the truth. He even knows that there is a kind of concern for souls which is only a form of self-discovery or self-importance. This is perhaps especially true of direction, because direction has the advantage for one's self-esteem that in the role of counsellor there is less demand for personal engagement, and the violent shocks of reality are mitigated. But he certainly does not remain passive. He knows what he has to do, and brings all his possibilities to bear, both of reason and of experience. But having done what is in him, he knows himself to be an unprofitable servant. He is almost astonished at success, marvelling at the work of God; but is not vexed by failures, knowing them to be inevitable and not believing that the Kingdom of heaven will be harmed by them. If it happens that his task is taken from him, he will not make difficulties about it.

Purity of Heart

When purity of heart is spoken of in the matter of direction, everyone thinks about the dangers of personal attachments. That is taking a limited view of things. In reality, purity of heart is the acquired habit of transparency in relation to God, which means that in his actions, decisions, and relationships with others, a man is not deceived by his secret motives and submits them more and more to the light of God.

It is this disposition which makes possible the action of the Holy Spirit, an action which, because it does not encounter the interferences of irritability, jealousy, self-esteem, and everything else that obscures our true vision, is able to make itself felt in the spirit of the director. The latter's concern is not to conduct clever examinations so as not to be deluded by the things that happen. He proceeds in fact more simply. He always tries to behave with complete rectitude before God; he acts according to his inspiration and proceeds.

In docility to events and to the unexpected. Because by these, God brings the instrument of his choice into the light of truth, so as to make him understand the source of his efficacity. From the way in which one person accepts ill health, another accepts an incapacity to work or extreme frailness, another a secret trial that no one else knows of, each learns to be detached from the trust he puts in himself and to lean only on God. He learns in concrete fashion to recognize the origin of all things, and not to sever the good from its source. This disposition is more important than anything else. Its absence prevents docility to the Holy Spirit, allows personal inspirations to be mistaken for the movements of God, and may result in that air of unassailable self-assurance possessed by the man who believes he has the Holy Spirit on his side because he thinks himself spiritual, evangelical, apostolic, or religious.

The best apprenticeship for that rectitude is life itself; our chance encounters, our slips, our mistakes. Everything is a means to this progress that never stops, and that we cease to make only on the day when we believe it to be assured. A real emptying of the self which opens us to enlightenment. A more radical demand than the accumulation of prayers, works, acts of penitence. It is the most indispensable thing for those whose mission it is to work for the Kingdom of God, especially in the depths of other hearts. The more delicate the task, the finer the instrument must be.

Clearly, in this process of refinement a special part must be accorded to the purification of the feelings. Many apostles remain ineffective, or to a great extent have their hands tied, through the absence of purification. But it is important that the problem should be correctly stated; many resolve it by fear or by flight, believing that they are required to have no feelings, or to repress their emotional reactions. But we are still very much the slaves of our feelings if we have to take notice of them to that extent. The reactions that occur in them in contact with things and persons are not in themselves an obstacle to our transparency towards the grace of God. They are natural, and as such, good. Purification consists in not allowing ourselves to be enclosed within the movement that we feel, not to enjoy it for ourselves, but to rise above it on light wings and with it commit ourselves to God. The apostle cannot prevent himself from being sensible of the confidences he receives, or the quality of the souls which are opened to him. How can those he directs give him their trust if they do not meet with a sincere affection? But the detachment which the director exercises, in his love of God, to whom he has consecrated his chastity and in whom he strives to see all things, enables him to lift those he meets above the present moment. What detaches him is not a movement of repression of his feelings, but a movement of perpetual opening, a ceaseless mounting towards other skies than the skies that nature shows.

This purification, because it is real, does not lead either to rejection or to neurosis. It may surely be said that since it reaches down to the deepest springs of a man's tenderness and affection, where in his freedom as a creature he has chosen to love his fellows in the love that creates them, it will allow him to achieve the perfect development of himself, and even to correct, more surely than would a medical treatment, the inevitable deviations to which all human affectivity is subject. "A truly supernatural spirit, the detachment which is the fruit of charity, an attention quick to gather the results of experience, the purification of the tendencies operated by the grace of God, will more than make up for what directors might have obtained by undergoing an analytical experience in the usual sense."[1]

It is this transparency of the heart and this unequivocal detachment that give the director his humanity and his assurance. They permit him audacities which are needful but sometimes disconcerting even to himself. They prevent him from spreading infatuation . . . the secret charm that enchains sensibilities and, even when possessed by generous people, makes adult choices impossible. They ensure the climate of mutual trust which banishes fear and reticence. The lives of the saints would provide us with thousands of examples of such effects, and we should perhaps be astonished to find the best of them among those who seem to be the most austere—the Desert Fathers. Purified hearts are free to love. Their love makes them sometimes impose acts of gentleness, and sometimes makes them demanding; but those who are

[1] Louis Biernaert, "Etudes Carmélitaines," *Direction Spirituelle et psychologie,* p. 324.

its objects never for a moment doubt the love that inspires this diversity. Nor could it ever be fear that impelled them suddenly to change direction. We are here at the summits of detachment, which are also the summits of love. To us who are far from that ideal, they show at least the road to follow.

The Peace of God

What those who are under direction today have perhaps most need to feel in their directors is that peace of God which, throughout all events, keeps them unperturbed, relaxed, and confident. Here is truly the disease of our time: "The nervous system is currently subjected to heavy strain by a civilization which fosters anxiety. Lack of confidence is not always a lack of good will on the part of the Christian, and is not necessarily the result of repeated negligences in religious matters. Intense anxiety is at times the consequence of some pathological state. . . . It is then difficult to preserve the calm which Christianity should logically maintain in every soul."[1] The director is one in whom the grace of God has been strong enough to calm the nervous tension that in others, as Scaller says, is preventing surrender to God.

This peace should be felt first of all in his prayer. It should be one of its principal effects. There is a certain anxious way of praying for others, and an anxiety about the concerns of the kingdom, which have nothing to do with the "solicitude" of St. Paul for the Churches entrusted to him. There enters into it a great deal of the natural anxiety that fills our contemporaries in regard to the world and the future of humanity. It is normal for a director to feel this anxiety, as others do. Perhaps he will never be free of it, and in a sense his incapacity is good, because it

[1] Scaller, *Direction des âmes et médecine moderne,* Paris, 1959.

allows others to recognize themselves in him. But men must equally be able to see the light of the peace that shines in the darkness enveloping him and them. They must be able to catch hold of the divine patience which the priest learns from his daily meditation on Scripture, and which will ultimately triumph over fear. They must find in him the certainty St. Peter speaks of, which assures us when we are impatient with the evil surrounding us that it is not God's will "that any should perish, but that all should reach repentance" (2 Pet. 3, 9).

Certainly, it is good to pray for those who are in our charge, and to seek in our prayer for the advice we should give them. But this search is not always sure in its results as to the soundness of the advice—an effort of reflection might perhaps have enabled us to arrive at it more happily—and it should be its principal aim to establish the heart in peace and serenity, so that it can say without haste or hurting too much, the thing that is hard to hear or delicate to explain. Even if the person consulting us does not take away soothing words, or a ready-made solution to a problem that does not have one, or that only the person himself can resolve, he will at least have glimpsed through us the God of peace. Something of the director's patience will have passed to him, calming his hurry and purifying his conceptions of the Kingdom, which was above all what he needed.

Here is the spirit in which a number of the suggestions made in the second part of this chapter should be put into practice. True, they are useful on the merely human level in helping us to achieve real attention to others. But they are much more so when we understand that real attention is a spiritual relaxing that makes us responsive to the Holy Spirit's unceasing activity in each and all of us, even though in our efforts to do everything ourselves we are hardly conscious of it. And then we soon come to see that this interior plasticity is opening us to an extraordinarily real world, that of the grace of God, which sustains its action through all the years and the wanderings of a human life.

There could scarcely be a more priestly task than this, which makes us collaborators with the Spirit of God, and allows us to contemplate its endless workings throughout the world.

The prayer that the director prays to God for those entrusted to him is both an entreaty like that of Abraham and Moses, and is also that of the prophet and above all of Christ, who seeks to identify Himself wholly with the Father's will for every man's salvation. Prayer for others is more than an anxious prayer about their destinies. It is a prayer which binds us in the depths to God, and makes us capable of seeing, through darkness and disaster, how God leads all towards the light and brings good out of evil. It establishes us in peace to receive the other, because it bathes us in hope and makes us love as God loves.

There are many directors who need these long hours of prayer and meditation on the Scriptures, not as an escape from a harsh world or from the grip of anxiety, but to learn, as St. John of the Cross expresses it, not to compromise divine action by their indiscreet haste, with its pressure for immediate results. God does not hurry; a thousand years for him are as a day. One might say that it is the devil who is always in a hurry, because his time is limited.

This peace, the fruit of prayer and faith, reassures the director in the demands that he must make. Scripture teaches him that many things can be understood only by doing them, and he must allow the doing to unfold its benefits. The event does more good than our explanations or our attempts to go over the ground again. But it is hard at times to be silent, like the father in the parable, and allow the beloved son to go his way! We should prefer to be sure, or to avoid the difficulty. At moments like this we must feel that God acts, and let him work things as he wills. It is enough that at the hour of trial the sufferer should find us on his road, waiting for him, as the father waited for the prodigal, in the certainty of our faith. And may this also teach us never to be surprised by anything, to listen, to say the same things over again without ever growing tired of the recital of failures, even the most unexpected ones, and to await God's hour, even if it were the last.

This peace, it should be said, must be directed towards ourselves as well. People always say, Do what you can and then leave it to God. But this must never be said with an air of resignation, almost of despair. Inevitably our task, which remains human, involves with it the deceptive question: Shouldn't I have done something different? And then, one never knows how things are going to turn out. Faced with this world of freedom, how can anyone prevent himself from feeling extremely clumsy and impotent? Even years of experience will not guarantee us against making mistakes. We are collaborating in the work of God, but the will of God escapes us. Then we have two contradictory feelings at once: on the one hand the certainty that it is God's will for us to do something or other this very day, and on the other hand the feeling that it is beyond our understanding, which keeps us in an attitude of listening and looking. It is not a bad thing that the one we are directing should feel us being caught up in this double movement; he can draw assurance from it, although he can never rest in it. It is the Holy Spirit who is leading both master and disciple, so that even if we should happen to find ourselves faced with an obvious error on our part, we do not keep on worrying about our failure. We remember once again that God brings good out of evil.

Largeness of Heart

It really needs a large heart to undertake such a role: both breadth of views and absence of susceptibility. The director must feel himself to be above the ups and downs of existence, even while he is living it in all its details with love. He must never allow himself to be hampered by the petty judgments of those who always have an opinion about what he is doing, and do not fail to communicate it; nor to insist upon any privilege, being free as he is from official function. Independent, but without haughtiness or spite. Happy, even if the good he has hoped for is brought about by another.

This work of direction, which should open the heart to the infinite breadth of the Spirit, seems to turn some people into busybodies, anxious, inquisitive, touchy. Why is it that directors, who are concerned with the good of others, should be on the lookout for the smallest fuss, or panic over futile gossip? They feel themselves ceaselessly obliged to interfere. They run around after meetings that the people involved in them often do not want. They cannot admit that those they direct should wish to leave them and go to someone else.

These are very human faults, the mark of small minds or unenlightened zeal; but they also indicate the absence of real love. Or rather, those who react like that are loving themselves without knowing it, and wanting to find themselves in those they direct. The marks of attention they give to others are aimed only at reassuring or comforting themselves. This is the way that cliques and coteries begin. Direction then attains just the opposite goal from the one it sets itself: it is tyranny in the name of God, instead of freedom.

Magnanimity lived out to its ultimate consequences leads to the attitude of Christ, who was reviled and did not open his mouth, and in the certainty of his cause and his strength, resisted evil with good and put himself in the Father's hands. In this feeling that no one is necessary to anyone, when we are as alone as Christ was on the Cross, we discover the workings of universal salvation and become disposable for greater tasks.

4. APTITUDE AND CAPABILITY

Do these unreasonable demands for the composition of a real director defy us, and condemn us never to meet such a treasure? It is true that spiritual direction seems to be the confluence of all sorts of qualities, human and divine, which can rarely come together among men, even the most saintly. Have we in fact with our ideal reached an unattainable limit?

It is true! A director is a gift of God, and the aptitude which makes him equal to his task is a real "charisma." For one who has received it, there are no questions. It is easier to do than to explain. The one who does not have it loses himself in analysis, and finds in the advice he is given only complications which, applied to the letter, make him clumsy and artificial.

Should we then despair of being able to train a man who could come anywhere near the ideal? Actually, everyone carries this unapproachable ideal in his heart; it is that of a being unified by the transcendence of the work to which he is given. It is therefore among those who tend in peace towards this interior unity that there is the chance of finding the best directors. They are the sages in the ancient and biblical sense of the word. It may be that we shall be more likely to meet them among the simple than the learned. At least it will be necessary for the learned to have rediscovered simplicity. Throughout the Church's history, there have always been such simple women or lay brothers who were consulted by everyone. Like that woman St. Ignatius tells of in his autobiography, who said to him one day, "May it please Our Lord to appear to you."[1] People like this seem to possess from the very first that candor in the face of reality, that capacity for wonder, that absence of self-seeking which are qualities so necessary to the director, but which seem to him at first so remote from the training to which he must bind himself.

It must be said: the conditions of modern life, which have become the conditions of apostolate, do not favor the discovery and training of this kind of man. We seem to have lost the feeling of spontaneity. In the individual as well as the professional life, everything has to be planned and prepared in advance. If man encloses himself in this world of precision and technique, it kills inspiration. There is no room left for the free world of thought, spirit, and self-giving. The apostolate itself is in danger of becoming simply an application of techniques. In these rules of ours there is no place for spiritual direction, as there is none for human, personal relationships. We, who are so concerned for autonomy, are possibly jeopardizing the formation of persons. A certain attitude to existence and apostolate nullifies in advance the conditions for the development of the spiritual life, because man is no longer searching for unity in the Spirit, but in recipes and pure technique. Love itself becomes degraded, and becomes mere sexuality.

A director, then, can be formed only in the measure that personal experience is possible to him, because experience alone reveals aptitude and shows the individual's capabilities.

How is his potential to be discovered in experience? By find-

---

[1] St. Ignatius adds that, taking the remark literally, he was staggered by it. There was true wisdom on the part of this humble woman.

ing occasions for its exercise. Can they be created? What would be said of a surgeon who practiced on his patients? The truth is that in this as in everything else there are revealing tastes, and some temperaments are more apt than others. It would be a worth-while undertaking were a study made to determine which kinds of temperament are best suited to spiritual direction. In such a case, scientific work would be placed at the service of the Spirit.

In any case, when the bent for it has been recognized, there should be no fear of trying it out. Seeking the advice of experienced elders, and studying their methods of procedure, we shall find the best safeguards against going astray. The student watches operations being performed before trying his hand at them. We listen to the talk of others to improve our own command of speech. And this domain, where charisma and the freedom of the Spirit hold sway, is in no wise to be entered casually. Even if after watching someone else's methods we decide that we should not do things in the same way, it is good to have studied them for a long time in order to make them our own. It is through these contacts that we are revealed to ourselves. We must be prepared for a great deal of looking on and asking questions.

There will be a chorus of complaints: I am alone, on my own, with nothing but my observations and my books. The objections are well founded. But it is just because of this that I have a dream of spiritual centers, grouping together directors of seminaries, preachers of spiritual exercises, practitioners of direction, men engaged in apostolic activity, all who are desirous of fidelity to the demands of the Holy Spirit and are united in this one ideal. It is in this way that a tradition is built up, from which real spiritual directors may one day be developed, people who have the charisma for it. The ground will have been prepared.

And in fact, almost everywhere, such grounds exist. Meetings, sessions, publications, and group researches all go to prove it. Their very multiplicity tends to overwhelm anyone who is trying to keep up to date. Swamped with his work, with advice, with points of view, he hardly knows which way to turn, and can never find time to be himself. Once more we come up against the need for a personal training, to bring all these things within the individual's reach, and make a unity of them.

Without question, to preserve the unity underlying the various points of view and the ideas which are piling up on all sides, and above all to preserve a hierarchy of values among them without which real unity will be lacking, nothing is more useful for the individual than to have had a personal experience of direction. Not as a scholar might learn and judge, but as a disciple of the Spirit who is practicing under a master. And here, inevitably, we must mention the benefits of the *Spiritual Exercises* for those who are charged with the work of spiritual direction.[1] There are so many points of view and unrelated ideas which fall into place in studying them. After this experience we no longer see things in the same way. Everything has been simplified.

In any case, it must be said that just as every priest is called to preach, with more or less good fortune, so every priest in varying degrees is called to direct. He will have to discover through experience his grace, his place, and his individual style. It is quite certain that no one can teach him these things; each

[1] In his encyclical *Mens Nostra* of December 20, 1929, Pope Pius XI, speaking of spiritual exercises, said of St. Ignatius's book that it had gained "distinguished acceptance as the wisest and most universal code for leading souls to perfection." Naturally on condition that they are not twisted, even under pretext of strict fidelity to the letter, the *Spiritual Exercises* constitute, by their balance and their dynamism, one of the best ways of forming priests to the task of spiritual direction.

must discover them for himself. Everyone is not made for every-one, and there are directors who are well adapted to one group and unsuited to another. Somewhat the same thing happens among doctors. Specialization is a necessity of life, as it is inscribed in nature. The essential thing is to recognize it and not choose it haphazard. But whatever may be each individual's speciality, there is one quality which must be common to all, for it is this that makes the director; it is the profound unity of the person.

Every one of us preserves the memory of a priest who has influenced him. He may not perhaps have had outstanding knowledge; his psychology was limited, and we could see its deficiencies; his teachings were those of his time and were not particularly original. We might even have been able to discover more saintly directors than he. But what we had before us was a man. He trained us more by what he was than by what he said or knew. With him, we had the feeling that we were alive. There was dialogue between man and man. We must always come back to this: this man is the real director. He is not undiscoverable. To find him and be like him both at once is the unity at which we must aim.

CHAPTER FOUR

The Kinds of Spiritual Direction

MANY people are uneasy in face of thinking which seems to them to be generalized or traditional. They give their attention only to the particular cases they meet every day. This natural preference inclines us often to seize on the minor aspects of things instead of responding to the real needs of those who come to us. It is taking the line of least resistance. That is the direction we must never follow when it is a matter of forming a man, and more especially a Christian. This observation dominates everything we have to say on the subject of the various types of help.

1. THE PERSON AND WHAT HE CAN BEAR

Adaptation to an environment is necessary, but constitutes only a first step in spiritual training. We have to adapt to the person, so that he in his turn can adapt freely to his environment and play his own part in it. We priests are always afraid—it is the defect of a quality—of not saying the right word, of not suggesting the right course of action. Without our being aware of it, the things we say are tributaries of what we are or of the work we do.

The real director is not the one who draws up a balance sheet at the end of the year of the candidates he has sent to the seminary, or recruited into some movement or congregation. With no preconceived ideas, and even taking care not to impose anything whatever, his first concern is to bring each individual face to face with his freedom and with God. Our work is to put the other on his guard against ill-judged undertakings, possible illusions or shortcomings, so that the Creator may freely "embrace His creature,"[1] and reveal His will to him. This principle of conduct is a golden rule.

Let us, therefore, lay down the following principle: Everyone, in a common Christian vocation, is not called to follow the same road. To help each to discover the way that is right for him, we have to respect in him, as the first signs that God gives him of His will, his condition, his age, his temperament, and the grace he has received. One will go to God in one way, another in another. "I wish that all were as I myself am," said St. Paul, on the subject of virginity. "But each has his own special gift from God, one of one kind and one of another" (1 Cor. 7, 7). This principle is valid for every commitment, and is fundamental to all spiritual direction.

The principle has its complement in the one following: Let everyone go from us in peace, because the advice he has received respects his nature and the grace of the moment. Often, so much damage is done by encouragements lavished without discernment, and supported by comparisons like "Why shouldn't you do as So-and-So does?" They discourage the person who is invited to make the parallel, and does not at the moment feel ready for

[1] "The Director must not turn or incline towards one side or another; but finding himself in balance between the two like a pair of scales, he must allow the Creator to act without intermediary on the creature, and the creature with his Creator and Lord." *Spiritual Exercises,* no. 15.

the course suggested. He then either resigns himself to remaining mediocre, as he believes he is, or else, so as not to lose face, under-takes an effort that hardens him. Such exhortations are useful only if they are brought to bear on people who are already ma-ture, have adult personalities, and perhaps a tendency to let them-selves be. They give them the idea of a higher call. Generally speaking, it is better, as in all education, to go in the direction of a person's qualities, or his grace, so as to give him confidence and encourage him in his first efforts. We run the risk of his break-ing later pledges if we mark his first attempts with an absolute and abstract character. In our impatience for tangible results we are like those parents who stifle a son under the image of the person they would like him to become. God knows what false or unhappy personalities such pressures have molded! There are pledges given in school, in the seminary, or in a novitiate which produce the same effect. It is very difficult to go back on them afterwards, because it would seem to show a lack of generosity. Besides, there is such social pressure that it would not be possible.

Even where precepts imposed by law are concerned, we must keep to the same procedure. Not that we should allow ourselves to pick and choose. The law is what it is, and it is good and spiritual (see Rom. 7). But our task is precisely to teach men to carry it out with love and in grace. There are rigid ways of ob-serving it which condemn our efforts to failure. Besides, for each one of us as for the people of God, there is a progressive way of being submitted to its demands. "You cannot bear everything at once," we might often say to those generous souls who are ready for any sacrifice but are burdened with a heavy past. Allow the grace of God to embrace you little by little in its action. The es-sential thing is that in spite of numerous falls and setbacks you should still have hope, and that the line you follow should be upward.

Alongside the grace of the directed, of which we have just been speaking, there is that of the director. It would be serious if he were to ignore it, and imagine himself able to deal with anyone or anything. One man is better with adolescents, another with adults, another in people's homes, and another in some different environment, not necessarily the one in which he was born or which he most often frequents. It is by trying in various directions that each discovers what the Lord destines him to be. He will become aware of it through a kind of easiness which, in spite of his natural apprehensions, makes him no longer hesitant in action, and enables him to take matters in hand.

Specialization does not mean that we should refuse all contacts except those for which we are best suited. How could we discover our aptitudes without a variety of encounters? And then it is not good to be a man of one environment. But, without despising any of them, we know that we cannot do everything. It would be more profitable for us to ask people who have different work from ours intelligent and sympathetic questions. We shall find in them our necessary complements. Through our approaches to our various tasks we shall be meeting in depth, drawing enrichment from our mutual confrontations.

In the desire for adaptation to others and ourselves, a danger to be avoided is that of trying to plan everything in advance. How should we deal with a married man, a young man, a spinster, a nun, a priest? It is because they worry about this multiplicity of cases that some would like a manual that would give the answers to typical difficulties. Certainly, it is good that they should be thought about beforehand. Perhaps it is even better to have thought about the meaning of each state of life and all that it comprises. But if you are inclined to look for precise answers in your files, have you noticed how your questioner seizes on them? "You have only to . . . ," you say, and he, thinking the thing perfectly simple, takes possession of your formula and applies it, making you say something you never said, and then if it turns out badly, reproaches you for it, saying that it is your fault because he did nothing but follow your advice. What you both failed to do was to come together within the situation, and, in the light of the Gospel and of grace, search for the one answer that fitted the case and the right way of being faithful to it.

Never enclose anyone in a recipe, even if it seems easier to you and him. Never impose from without a rule that has not been understood. It is good to advise someone to say his prayers every day, but if the practice is not accepted from within it is like those gymnastics courses that you follow because you see somebody else doing them, but which are of no value to you. The common rules are good, but it is the spiritual father's part to find out with each individual how they concern him and how he himself is to live them.

We must in fact pass beyond the recipes and practices, which are always useful as limbering exercises of general application, and lead the individual on to his own vocation, so that he may be able to adapt our advice to his special needs. Every practical solution must be born out of the existing positive elements contained within the subject himself. This method will not immediately produce spectacular results, but they will be positive because the method is truer. After all, if we are dealing with someone who has given up practicing or is having marital difficulties, we shall not expect him to start taking the sacraments the very next day, or to adopt at once a rigid fidelity that for the moment seems to him impossible. We shall go along with him in the actual situation in which he is, trying to help him to master it in its entirety. We must keep on bringing him back to the essential thing, which is what might be called the dynamic of his being. The solidity of the results will be our consolation one day for this austere and long-sustained patience.

In this slow progress, one of those you direct may accuse you of not understanding him, and another may unleash on you his pent-up bitterness against some law of the Church that has led him, as he thinks, into his present dilemma. Let him talk, go on loving him, and do not waste your time in trying to legitimize something that for the moment he cannot admit. Do not try to extort some gesture that he consents to for the sake of peace and quietness. Go on bearing with him the painful burden of the situation, and let him feel your firm and peaceful conviction that however long the road, you will come out into the light at last. You cannot tell him how, but you are quite sure of it. Even if you find that you have to refuse the sacrament, let it be with respect for the other's freedom, and never in such a way that he feels he is being despised or is driven to discouragement. Let him understand that the dialogue remains open so that he can find the way to freedom. And in the meanwhile, rejoice over the slightest progress made.

This kind of conduct is particularly important at the present time, when we often have to deal with unexpected, tangled, or even insoluble cases. To act otherwise is to turn aside those who have most need of us, and to leave ourselves surrounded with a little group of people who have never had to face great difficulties in their lives, or have become set in religious conformism.

Being open to everyone is much more important than having an exact knowledge of the environment where the one you are directing lives, or making a precise study of his case. It is this openness that explains the astonishing radiance of certain priests. They are consulted by Christians and non-Christians alike, because their smiling and comprehensive humanity, while not making light of any of the Christian demands, spreads confidence to all who meet them. We could say that behind the passing image we give them of ourselves, they see us in the light of the end to which we are moving. They listen attentively to our difficulties, but often they do not give us an answer, because there is none except to draw us beyond the level at which the problems are situated. How different from those anxious, restless priests who pass on their feverish anxiety to everyone who comes near them! There is no comfort in them, or if they try to give any it will be false comfort, that wants to hide the difficulties or is afraid of making you suffer. They have not gone down into the depths of the love with which God surrounds all his creatures, and their disquiet is imparted to us, but not the strength to bear it.

2. OCCASIONAL DIRECTION

We must be willing, as mentioned in the second chapter, to give help in passing to an individual who is usually helped by someone else. Occasional help of this kind is one of the most frequent occurrences in spiritual direction. Here as in physical life, all sorts of influences normally come into play to guide a person to maturity. Each of us must be prepared to act at his hour, and then when the time has come, to pass on the work without jealousy or bitterness to another. All we do must be inspired by a spirit of serene detachment and inner freedom.

What should be the director's concern on such occasions?

First of all there are the meetings in the confessional. The priest may ask questions and must give an admonition. If he is the one to whom confession is occasionally or even regularly made, but is not the person's director, he should not ask too many questions. There is a way of questioning that both relieves the conscience of the priest and puts the penitent at ease: "Do you have a director? Have you talked to him about these difficulties? Do you find he is able to give you sufficient enlightenment?" The answers will dictate your conduct. It is obviously contra-indicated, if the penitent is at peace, to go against the advice of a habitual director or to show our disagreement. We are there only to administer the sacrament, and to be unwearied in giving confidence to those who have recourse to our ministry. Many excellent Christians hesitate to go and confess to some particular priest who is not their director, because they dread indiscreet questions, or an admonition that misses the point, or else have no wish to give all over again the same explanations about the past. This does not mean that the confessor should be content to offer general or lifeless comments, but that he should simply allow a word of light and peace to come from his heart.

Arising from that first observation, a number of questions suggest themselves. For example: How to behave towards a person who confesses a fault that he does not dare to admit to his usual director? Should he be urged to do it? It might be more useful to help him to clarify the motive for his reticence. Why is he afraid to speak? From the tenor of his answers we may perhaps be able to prime a work of liberation that goes further than the particular difficulty we found to begin with. In a word, whatever the occasion, we must be less attached to the material fact than to its significance in the whole life-pattern.

From the solution of this case we may state a general rule:

Take advantage of every encounter with Christians who are passing through your hands to collaborate in the great work of liberation that the Holy Spirit is accomplishing in them. Instead of weighing them down with ready-made formulas or dull practices, encourage them to see how every Christian life becomes interiorized and unified. Instead of listening to detailed and routine lists of self-accusations, made out of boredom or fear, let us teach the continuity of an effort made in the love with which God surrounds us. Using all the necessary discretion, and perhaps even keeping within the framework of the confessional, we might give a new direction to those Christian lives which would transform them and set them on the road to a personal religion.

Again, we must take advantage of these occasional encounters to reveal to a person something he needs without knowing it. Perhaps he is accusing himself habitually of the same faults. He will possibly gain more from getting things into clear focus as a result of a conversation that we suggested to him at that time, than he would from a wearisome and profitless recourse to the sacrament. An interview would at least allow us to bring out into the open what it is he is accusing himself of, and to place his responsibility before God. Numbers of people live in anxiety about the whole question of chastity because they have never had a chance of being enlightened in this way.

As well as this occasional help during a confession or in the course of a conversation, there is the other kind which consists in helping someone to have a spiritual experience such as a retreat. Unless we are to regard it simply as a series of meetings, a priest cannot perform his part in a retreat without assuming the responsibility of direction. It is normal for him to propose it to those who are making the retreat with him, even if they have a regular director. But this kind of direction will require of him a great deal of both clarity and detachment. The clarity is needed to say what the regular director, who is not there to see how the directed person evolves under this type of experience, cannot or will not know how to say. The detachment is needed because the director must not be tempted to push direction beyond the limits of the retreat, and above all must not show any trace of astonishment if during the retreat itself one of those present fails to understand what is being offered to him, or just slips away. The ideal in these cases is that there should be an understanding, to the advantage of the person directed, between the regular and the temporary directors. That does happen sometimes, and the gains are immense. It is like a consultation between the general practitioner and the specialist.

Let us add, by way of conclusion to this point, that it can be useful to a director to exercise his ministry in both ways at once, the regular and the occasional. He will understand better how to conduct himself in the two situations, and will gain a clearer appreciation of their different focuses.

3. COLLECTIVE DIRECTION

Direction is not accomplished only through personal dialogue, although this is generally implied. It is often begun, clarified, and developed in communal meetings, retreats, and life-reviews. Which is another way of saying that direction, though personal in its essence, must not become jealously enclosed in itself.

There are two typical kinds of such help: that of the group and that of the retreat. The group, whether it listens to a talk or engages in a discussion, has often the effect on personal direction of giving it a dimension and an openness that it might otherwise perhaps never have achieved. It requires us to meet the demands of objective, unimaginary facts; it imposes confrontation with others, with events, persons, and things. Only to be profitable, this confrontation must leave the door open to personal conversations, in which the questions that were not asked, or that the group asked in crude forms, will receive individual replies. There is a delicate interplay here, of which the priest, sharing in the life of the group, must be aware so as to allow it the possibility of happening.

The same could be said of the retreat. Ideally, one could dream of individual retreats, perfectly adapted to each person's development. But these are perhaps only possible in special circumstances, like those of a vocation for example, or for people who have reached sufficient human and spiritual maturity. In practice, most retreats are collective. For personal direction to be possible, it is at least to be hoped that the number of participants should never be so large, the timetable so crowded, or the atmosphere so stifling that individual exchanges are practically ruled out. There are retreats that are so overloaded with meetings, exercises, and lectures that you might think they were sessions for psychological conditioning. When, on the other hand, they take place in a relaxed atmosphere and with respect for the individual, collective retreats, especially if they bring together people who are almost untrained or in the course of training, have the advantage of presenting on a small scale and in one happening, the rules of all true direction. Many of the points developed in talking to a group could not be brought out with the same force, or in so clear a way, in a private conversation. It only remains then for each listener to apply them to his personal case.

Group exchanges, or the teachings of a retreat, are not substitutes for personal direction, but they broaden it and allow it to go more quickly to work. The progress that is taking place today in what is called "group dynamics,"[1] far from contradicting the traditional point of view about direction, can only purify it from what there may be in it of an equivocal, narrow or self-concerned nature. An agreement like this between complementary points of view demands that neither the upholders of personal dialogue nor the promoters of collective discussion should become set in a formula, under pretext of having themselves found advantages in it that they had not found elsewhere. This necessary focussing will purify each position, if it tries to insist on its uniqueness, of its naïve or illusory elements.

Here as elsewhere, we must not want to do everything at once, or take everyone along the same road. The essential thing is not to have belonged to a particular group, or to have been directed by a particular person—in both cases this would be nothing but worldliness—but to become docile to the Holy Spirit in the totality of one's being. All the rest, groups, retreats, direction, are only means.

4. DIRECTION BY CORRESPONDENCE

Some people ask what to think of direction done through letters. One has only to look through the bookshelves of a library to realize that this kind has never at any time been short of advocates. Among Christians and non-Christians alike, it has become a literary form.

Its inherent danger is that we see ourselves writing, and judge ourselves in the eyes of posterity, or simply those of the person we are writing to. Complacency and artifice in either case.

[1] A concise summary of the theory and practice of group dynamics is given by W. W. Meissner, S.J., in his *Group Dynamics in the Religious Life* (Notre Dame, 1965).

Nevertheless, we have to recognize that distance often makes this exchange necessary. No doubt if it is to be profitable, it should be founded on quite a long direct acquaintance, and should find renewal from time to time in conversational contacts. If that can be assured, the exchange of letters is a practical means of preserving the necessary unity and continuity in one's self-conduct. With letters, there is no need to keep on repeating the same explanations. A word is enough for us to understand one another, and that is an immense advantage.

In assessing its truth, we should no doubt employ the same criteria as for all direction: Is the exchange moving in the direction of openness and progress? Is it leading to greater simplicity? It is certain that the director must be exigent enough with the other, and free enough with himself, for a vain correspondence to cease of its own accord.

Perhaps this suggestion will prove valuable: that in reading a letter the director should not allow himself to be impressed by the details, but should receive as a whole the message addressed to him. The aggregate impression will dictate his reply. The latter should be couched in direct, almost swift, language, and should be faithful to the first intuition that was produced in him by the impact of the initial reading. Only, so that he is not misled by first impressions, let them be noted if need be as soon as the letter is received, and then he can allow several days to elapse before sending off his reply. Thus he will reap the combined advantages of his first flash of inspiration and of the distancing afforded by the delay. Or even if he decides to make a rough draft, he will be constrained to calm down his emotional reactions and this will give him rather more chance of taking his distances. The procedure has a further advantage: we can keep a copy of what we have written, and in many cases that is useful.

5. PERMANENT DIRECTION IN SOME CASES

As soon as we begin to examine individual cases, it is principally negative advice and cautions that come to mind. How could it be otherwise, when we see the disasters produced by those who go to work too quickly, or are all agog to apply the principles they have been taught or have once succeeded with? Our counsels will look like needless guardrails to people who have no practical experience, and will be of little use to those who have.

Youth

For many priests, young people constitute almost the only field in which they can exercise direction. And it is at this age that the objective of direction is most limited, because what has then to be done above all is to lay the human foundations for it, and these depend only partly on the priest. They are the work of the family, the group, the environment, and the school.

That is why it is so important for a priest who is concerned with the direction of young people to be intimately connected with their environment, and to be playing an active part in it himself. This can be well seen in a college, where the spiritual father is participating in the life of the whole body and is interested in the smallest details of that life. The same rule applies to all the forms of ministry in which, practically, the beginnings of spiritual direction are possible only to the extent that the priest is dealing with the group to which the adolescent belongs. Direction finds its point of departure in the demands of group life. The link, however, becomes less necessary in proportion as a young man outgrows his adolescence and is capable of a personal life.

From this point of view, we can understand why educators are so anxious to arrange what we might call common spiritual direction at the center of a communal society. It consists in uniting all their efforts in a definite direction so as to influence the activities of the group and the individual. Personal spiritual direction finds its place within this greater whole.

A schema for that kind of collective direction must take most careful account of what psychology has to say about the stages of evolution of childhood and adolescence, so that we may not rush through them heedlessly. A similar effort is being progressively made in religious education, with the object of turning it into something more than a simple matter of absorbing ready-made formulas. Let us hope that the same thing will happen throughout the whole of the spiritual education properly so called of the child and the young man. In this development, teams of school teachers and chaplains have a most important part to play.

Researches have been made on the various aptitudes that different characters show for the development of a religious life. These character studies, which clarify for the individual the efforts he will need to make in order to unify his personality, are much more useful in the directing of young people than they would be for adults. They prevent us from being unduly impressed by the greater or lesser degree of facility or difficulty that a person has in relation to the moral life. They also help us in drawing up with him a balance sheet of the materials at his disposal for his self-construction, in the same way that we try to help him to become conscious at a fairly early age of his physical evolution.

The danger would lie in expecting too much from these studies, and so enclosing ourselves within the framework of a purely human education, following the example of the counsellor who decides in which subjects a child has the best chance of succeeding. The direction of the person begins from the moment when we have passed the stage of psychological determinism, and have reached that of his free determinations and the movements of the Holy Spirit in him. It is very certain that the Spirit is at work in the child as in the adult, and adapts Himself to his mentality. The good director is simply the one who discerns the work of grace underlying the normal efforts that everyone must put forth, and helps the child to attune his conduct to it.

People often behave with children or young folk as though they did not believe in this secret work of grace. They try to produce from them a kind of religious behavior which looks reassuring at the time, but which has disconcerting results, particularly at the difficult age. The work of grace has never been taken seriously. They believe only in what can be measured and felt. If the essential foundations are lacking, we can hardly be surprised when the rest, however well-built it seems to be, is carried away by the storm. At this age, spiritual direction is simple and almost rudimentary in its manifestations, but is such as to permit the emergence of grace from within the searches and developments of adolescence. It will be unlikely to insist on a multitude of practices; still less will it seek to ward off dangers or prevent the inevitable evolution. It will remain unperturbed by weaknesses or resistance, and will make use of all circumstances to prepare a soil where grace may flourish.

Vocations

The above remarks are particularly relevant in the case of vocations. We may sin in regard to these by doing too much or too little. There is a lot of random talk about them, but it is not by talking that we shall help, so much as by providing a climate that will allow their disclosure. The opposite mistake is to believe that at an early age desires for a higher life are not to be taken seriously.

The essential thing is not to talk but to develop freedom, desirous only of God's will. The decision will come of itself at the right time, if our care has been to make it possible. The preparation of a balanced human being takes place on all levels simultaneously, through confrontation with life, with others, and particularly through relationships with the opposite sex; but it must never be forgotten that grace is performing its secret work in this soul that has not yet achieved maturity, or is struggling with numerous emotional conflicts. We may be favorably impressed with the results obtained, and then we must be on our guard against pushing the individual into a premature decision. It is for him to feel that the moment for taking it has come.

Until he has reached that moment, it will be better to continue with his ordinary training, advising him about an examination he could prepare for, or a trade he could learn, anything that increases his usefulness in one way or another and confronts him with the demands of reality that every man has to meet. During this time he can be helped by an enlightened spiritual life to discern little by little the false motives for his actions, even those that are most generous in appearance. He must learn not to run away from himself even in humiliating situations. Lucidity of this kind is not to be acquired in a few months. It requires much confidence and openness. But it will eventually enable the decision to be made as easily as one picks a ripe fruit.

In this sphere, directors must be warned against using the argument of generosity. It is easy to use it, and as easy to be deceived by it. It is unwise to employ it unless it is brought to bear at exactly the right moment, that is to say, when and where

God wants us and grants us grace enough to act in peace and trust. So long as there is an accompaniment of tension and anxiety, the director can give no credit to the decisions it inspires. He must then try to discover the motives for the tensions or fears: self-seeking, pride, or resentment.

At moments like this, many directors are afraid of losing a vocation. Their fear is passed on to the person they are directing, to his greater harm, for it amounts to an unconscious restriction of his freedom. Even when the issue lies close to his heart, the director must achieve within the one he directs a state of royal indifference, not desiring one thing more than another, either priesthood or marriage, but ready to choose in this way or that according to the will of God. "At one time," a seminarist said, "I wanted to be a priest. Now I want to do God's will, which is that I should be a priest."

Above all, when the time has come, he should consider the choice as the conclusion of a supernatural work, and not as the result of a merely rational examination of aptitudes and appropriate reasons. The choice remains the work of freedom under grace which enlightens and suggests. Our part is to prepare for it; but when it is to be made, we should stand aside. The pupil must never be able to reproach us afterwards with having in the slightest degree influenced his decision.

Among the counsels that make a choice possible, there is one of special importance: a decision is not valid if it is reached in a state of crisis. The same must be said about those that result from the fugitive desires which assail the individual during the difficult years, when he is trying himself out in all directions without being able to fix on any of them. The peace of the decision, or the feeling of peace that accompanies the birth of the first idea, is an essential element in judging a vocation. From this point of view, more credit can be given to vocations chosen during the quiet years of childhood than to those that emerge from the troubled hours of adolescence. And just as the director must not allow his influence to bear either on one side or the other, so he must be ever watchfully aware of the context of a decision, and bring it to the notice of the one he directs. Some will decide on a sudden impulse, while others abruptly abandon the road they have taken. In such cases, a director must clearly say that these procedures are not acceptable and in no way constitute acts of freedom. He must show the greater firmness because the other thinks himself free. Wait until he has calmed down and you will see. And in the meanwhile, do everything you can to retrieve him.

The director must not be precipitate. He must be able to sustain someone in his search, and give him all the time he needs. It may be a long time. Many people today experience prolonged adolescence, and this prevents them from making real decisions.

The Family

One of the questions greatly preoccupying priests in their ordinary ministry is that of the help which they should give in the home. The most important point to remember at the start is perhaps that Christians pledged in marriage do not expect a priest to have a solution for all their difficulties, or an exact knowledge of a situation he has not himself experienced. They expect to be understood and loved, treated as free and living persons, and not as abstract cases to which the law is to be applied. Above all, they ask for a father's prejudice in favor of his children who are not unwilling to obey but do not know what to do. In a word, priests and married people must discover together that the law which seems so hard is really a law of love, and how it must be borne in mutual love and in the love of God.

It is no use pouring out appeasing words that dodge the problems. Why refuse to look the real difficulties in the face? Every condition has its own, the priesthood like the rest. These difficulties must be accepted, simply, humbly, as we accept our own, —"Bear one another's burdens," says St. Paul, —realizing that it will take a long time to solve them, but knowing too that each difficulty overcome helps us to grow in love. We must never allow ourselves to be hardened by negative or legalistic attitudes. If there are some who think the Church has no understanding of men's difficulties, it is perhaps because we who represent her have remained on the outside of things. When we isolate some point of the law, we make it inhuman; for an understanding of it we shall need the light of our faith in its fullness. We must try to relate the detail to the whole. Otherwise we should be condemning men to a habitual heroism, and this is not the Church's intention, for she knows that her words are addressed to ordinary human beings and sinners and not to supermen. We must first help souls to live in the understanding of the whole Christian mystery and the grace of their baptism; we shall then be helping them at the same time to a fuller assumption of particular laws and, if they fail, not to be discouraged by failure.

Again, it is most necessary for the priest to have a broad idea of marriage, the Christian idea. He should not raise the bidding, as though his own vows of chastity prevented him from understanding married love. To the extent that he himself is living out his own chastity as a man, he will have no difficulty in understanding from within the married faithful who have recourse to his ministry. For them he is the minister and witness of the Church's mystery, and this reveals to him the greatness of marriage, which is to be the visible sign of the love of Christ and the Church (see Eph. 5, 25). The truly faithful followers of Christ are not mistaken here; they sense that a real priest is one with them in the human family, and that if he does not express God's matchless love in the same way as they do, he is living with them in the same reality.

This global and serene vision of things allows a priest to face up to the difficulties people bring to him. He sees them, not as a stumbling block, but as a means, though sometimes a painful one, of growth. How many married Christians, wives especially, regret that they do not pray as they used to! They say they have too much to do, and readily accuse themselves of neglecting what they believe to be their spiritual life. A firm and tranquil direction would open their eyes to the reality, which is that God is not to be found in an illusory return to the graces of the past, but in a loving submission to the present moment. If in the multiplicity of their duties and the unexpected events of life they find occasions for the total resignation of themselves, they will discover, in a far more real way than they could ever have imagined, the poverty of the Beatitudes, which is the only real way to find God.

Something else that people have to learn is how to accept one another, recognizing what it is possible to do together and what it is not. Some people dream of a spiritual life in common, in which all secrets would be shared. But for one thing, it is fitting that we should respect the part of God in another person, the invisible place which the Creator reserves for himself in his creature; and further, we must yield to the evidence that spiritual levels are different in each individual. A respectful silence in face of the other's mystery is one of the most beautiful expressions of love. It is an act of faith in the presence of God in them. And let it be strongly said, at difficult times it is the surest guard of love.

On the other hand, there are so many problems that can only be resolved together: those of continence, family planning, education. Just as the priest must be willing to give individual help to one who in his inward mystery is seeking the face of God, he should be just as unwilling, when these problems are brought to him, to help resolve them unless husband and wife are together. In this sphere, the only lasting solutions result from mutual agreement, or at least a tendency to agreement.

Faced with the admission of difficulties inherent in married life, we sometimes show an attitude that could be qualified as hardly Christian. As though it were sufficient to pass over a recipe and say, "Do this and don't worry." Technical methods, useful in their order, can never dispense a man from personal acceptance of his destiny. The ideal is not to get out of it lightly, with a bit of luck. That is unworthy of the sons of God. It is from within, from a total acceptance of the nature, commandments, and mystery of Christ, that the real solutions must come. Nothing defiles a man but what proceeds from his heart. It is to the heart that a priest must always return in helping others to grow as sons of God, in and through the accidents of an always unforeseeable path. His work is to deliver from anxiety and to give back hope, at the moments when those who come to him are lost in darkness and know the frequent humiliation of falling. So it is that he initiates them into the eternal beginning anew of the grace of God. This is a humbler but a truer way. It removes no exigencies, but simply banishes fear and leads to freedom.

In the help he gives to a married couple, a priest should not lose the sense of what might be called the vocation of the married state as such. It is dangerous for a pair to decide in advance that when they are married they will keep up the commitments they had before in some work or other. Trying to do this often becomes a source of friction, or at least of fatigue. The commitment, if it is to be continued, should be assumed together. Because it is no longer the individual but the couple who must bear witness in the life of the Church to the love that is in them. It is from their intimacy, from the experience they have of a true love, that they will draw the riches of their apostolic radiance. There are some women of good works who are so devoted outside the home only because they are running away from an intolerable marital situation. It is better to be less active and to have a warm and joyous presence. In the end, it is in this last kind of home, even if it is not devoted to any special work, that the Church is present.

Keeping to these principles of direction is relatively easy in relation to married people whom we see fairly often. Our task is more delicate when someone we do not know happens to bring up the problem of his conjugal life. He expects to be given a ready-made solution right away. If we allow ourselves to become involved in his problem, we shall either discourage him with our answers or anchor him in the idea that the Church understands nothing about the ordinary man. In these cases as in so many others we must remain humble, and guide the questioner as far as possible in the direction of faith, hope, and charity. At least we should try to open a door through which the Holy Spirit may one day be able to pass. Less than ever at such times should we allow ourselves to count up the "returns." The chances are that they will be illusory and will only flatter our vanity.

To help effectively in the home, a priest must have a profound sense of our common destiny as children of God, and must not believe that Christian perfection is reserved for privileged folk who have managed to avoid what the old-fashioned books call "the pitfalls of marriage." Moreover it must be as a priest that he manifests his esteem; that is to say, as a man who is conscious of the complementary values that are brought to married Christians by his priesthood and his chastity. To the extent that he himself is at ease in his vocation he will be able to confirm others in theirs, each respecting in all the grace of the one Lord and the mystery of the one Church.

Is it advisable for a married couple to have the same director? It is difficult to answer this question, because there are as many solutions as cases. The advantages and the drawbacks can easily be imagined. In any event, we may agree with Carré that "one supreme good must be safeguarded: freedom. However closely bound they may be by their legal and spiritual contract, however deeply united they may seem in the heart of the communal estate, husband and wife have free souls that God has created and the Saviour has redeemed. It is on God and on Christ that the soul depends; it is with God and Christ that it holds dialogue in a secrecy that none has the right to violate."[1]

The freedom that unites them they have received from God, and to God they owe the final homage for it. That is the secret that each respects in the other, taking care never to become a barrier between it and God. Far from being a cause of estrangement, it gives them a new reason for loving one another. For the secret is the presence of God, uniting them in what is beyond themselves. By ·it, the reality of their love is never enclosed in itself, but becomes a little more day by day the visible sign of the Church and of Christ, who is the surest foundation of their spiritual life.

[1] *Supplément de La Vie Spirituelle,* no. 34, September, 1955, p. 329.

Women

Spiritual direction in the home faces many a priest with the question of the particular attitude he should adopt towards women. At one time priests were taught an almost excessive reserve, women being presented to them as beings from whom they must protect themselves. A priest's manner nowadays will seem a little freer. He has, in fact, acquired broader and more open ideas, but he still remains vulnerable and not always at his ease in this sphere.

Undoubtedly, the priest would find the right note if he considered Christ's attitude towards the women He met in His ministry. It has nothing in it of rejection, contempt, or fear. There are shades of reserve and respect for the mystery of love that every woman bears in her, even when she is disfigured by sin. This is the center to which Christ clings, with the delicacy of the Creator who knows what there is in His creature.

The example of Christ allows the priest to establish himself little by little in an attitude of truth. It is from his chastity—that is, the special love he has vowed to the Lord, which unifies his human powers—that he draws an affection which is true, open, and full of naturalness.

There is, of course, the not infrequent case of the priest who, in the candor of his generosity, allows himself to be moved by confidences. In proportion as he abandons himself to this movement and does not control it, he unconsciously provokes in the other an inclination to add fuel to the fire, and this develops a process which is almost fatal. Naturally, it is often the best who are caught in this game. Some, who are preserved from danger by the banality of their spiritual life, are astonished to see others succumb to it, not having themselves reached the point where

158

the risk begins. And others again who are very unsure of themselves, taking refuge in what might be called premature flight, are so afraid of the trap that they fall into it.

The problem posed by the direction of women is in fact more the priest's than the woman's. Insofar as he himself is adult, and is attached to the Lord in the truth of his being, he will draw from the depth of his spiritual life the right inspiration to enable him as a man and a priest, without dallying and with respect, to help the woman to bring order into the flow of her intuitions and feelings. He will assure her insofar as he himself is untroubled. This conduct will require much patience of him, and reserve and real love at the same time. Little by little it will become spontaneous on his part, thanks to the maturity of his being as a man in the first place; but this would be ineffective unless there were joined to it the single-minded love that he has for Christ, which allows him not only to place others in His presence but to love them as they are, with all their wanderings and their woes.

Finally, the priest should never forget that one way of practicing St. Paul's injunction "Bear one another's burdens" is faithfully to keep everyone's secrets. This advice is specially important when the confidences of a married couple are involved. The priest should be an instrument of peace and concord. He is not called to sort out conflicts. "Who made me a judge between you?" said Our Lord to the two quarrelling brothers. Discretion alone permits the assumption of the role of counsellor.

Religious

The spiritual direction of religious women often demands a great deal of tact, since in many instances it cannot be definite.

This is so, in other words, because in many communities the practice of spiritual direction is also undertaken by the community's superior. In such often delicate situations, therefore, it is necessary for the priest and the superior, for the good of the subject, to work out a friendly arrangement, and this will usually involve a certain amount of restraint on both sides.

An agreement is impossible, for example, if the priest wants to interfere in everything, sides with one person or another, and becomes involved in community conflicts. Just as with quarrels between husband and wife, it is not his place to set himself up as a judge, but to help everyone concerned to discover the spiritual significance of each situation. Even so, he will not always be successful either in avoiding criticism or in not allowing himself to become involved in tendentious proceedings. At least let there be no attitude of conquest or overmuch self-confidence, to give these things a foothold.

At the same time, he should not consider his role as inferior or limited to the hearing of confessions. Undoubtedly, any thoughtful priest who has nuns in his charge will recognize that a superior is often better placed to give them the required guidance. But it is no less true that the nuns expect much of their priest, and are disappointed when they receive nothing from him. St. Theresa of Avila, who intervened without hesitation to repair the blunders of some of the priests who were directing her nuns, wished that both she and her daughters might meet with good directors. A priest should never be satisfied with the weekly utterance of banal little messages that he has prepared in advance. He should be ready to listen to a nun who seems to be out of the ordinary or difficult to understand, without depriving her by sharp or surprised comments of any desire ever to renew her confidences.

This supposes an esteem on his part for the religious life. There are priests who are perhaps afraid of approaching a world that they have never been taught to know. Some of them in any case see nothing in the religious life but its maladjustments or its incontestable littlenesses, and seem to ignore its value and the secrets of self-giving that it hides. When they hear nuns' confessions, they have the feeling that they are wasting their time. They can only deplore and criticize. The comparisons they make are always to the advantage of what is happening elsewhere, of people in the outside world, laymen, married people. The least one can say is that this is not the way to win the confidence of those whom one has a mission to help.

In fact, a real director of religious is a man who is almost astonished that he has such a responsibility, and is deeply respectful of the one he is directing. He does not try to assert himself, he listens and looks, but with intelligence and sympathy and without preconceived ideas. There is nothing about him of those directors who are more.like contractors than priests, and seem to find satisfaction in having all these souls in the yard. He does not seek to establish his rule or his methods. He does not imagine that he has a mission or any special competence. He does not impose plans of life. He simply loves Our Lord and the Church, and because his own spiritual life is simple, he says things as he sees them. He is not content with vague words, under the pretext that a nun should be satisfied with what she is given and is always enough for her. He encourages her to speak, but keeps his distance from the things he hears. His silences are a little disconcerting, until the day comes when he is sure he has understood, and he can make his demands and stick to them.

He himself is perhaps not a monk, and he may have thought

161

to start with that a monk would be better suited to the guidance of nuns. But he soon comes to see that this is not the real issue. A priest does not have to be married in order to help married people among the faithful, and neither does he have to be religious in order to understand the difficulties of other religious. The important thing is that here, as with married people, he should penetrate to the heart of things and their inner significance by the grace of his priesthood. He is not asked to resolve legal difficulties or to promote reforms, but to love and understand in faith.

Such a priest is a treasure for any community. He is the kind that every religious would wish to meet. Whether he speaks briefly or at length, his word goes directly to the heart and awakens what was asleep there. It inspires faith, light, and love. It is gentle even when it makes demands. It never offers recipes or tranquilizers. When it is unsure of itself, it remains silent. Of course, it is possible for a director like this to be troublesome, but if so, it is in a good way. He prevents positions from hardening, and meanness from spreading. If he has to make a break, he will do it without regrets. Knowing how to give his time and his heart, he preserves enough independence not to become identified with any party, and to be able to relieve genuine sufferings wherever they occur.

Priests

It is a fact that many priests find it embarrassing, not only to hear the confessions of their colleagues, but also to undertake to be their spiritual guides. Certainly, there is a good dose of human respect in this, but perhaps even more of awkwardness and inexperience. The priest simply does not know what to do.

Because he imagines that direction consists in superintending and giving orders, he dreads assuming this role in relation to someone who is his equal and knows him too well. The reaction is understandable. But he ought to try to grasp what it is that the priest who is coming to him expects, and his own needs should help him to do so.

What the priest needs in the first place is personal and brotherly help to restore his courage in the loneliness to which his existence often condemns him. There are times when in heaviness of heart he feels he is turning into a functionary, and is tempted to resign himself to the inevitable. It is then especially that the momentum of his spiritual life will weaken if he is not upheld by the intelligent and loving comprehension of an older man. He is not expecting answers; he wants someone to listen to him, and above all in a particular way. Spiritual solitude is his greatest danger. Even if it does not lead him into revolt or denial, it can deaden or harden him. The director, then, is someone to whom he can talk, candidly and in depth. When a service like this is asked of us, we should not run away from it under pretext of age, of business, or of incompetence.

Unfortunately, it is rare for a priest to have been trained for this kind of spiritual conversation. He often has an embarrassed memory of those, always slightly artificial, that he held with his director when he was at the seminary. They seemed to him at the time to be simply an article in the rules, to which he willingly submitted, but did not always feel to be necessary. Now, he feels that something is missing, but he does not know how to put it right.

He tries to find satisfaction in the team or the community. Priests often say, "We do not need a director. We are living as a team and sharing everything in common." There is a great deal of truth in this assertion. The fact that religious, living together, do not encounter any great difficulty in the matter of direction, shows precisely that they are receiving the best kind of training in this communal life. Spiritual direction is only its efflorescence, and the means of making it personal. This is something that cannot fail to develop by a process of natural evolution within the communities that are now everywhere being formed. The one does not go without the other, and it is to the advantage of both. A good director will reveal to an individual member the living forces that he can employ in the service of all.

Apart from this, why should we expect a priest to be able to find a director right on the spot? What will he do every time that he moves to a new post? If he has found a real director once in his lifetime, he need not bother to look for others. If their ways are parted by life, or death, he should be capable of living from the original impetus. A letter, a visit occasionally, will allow him to refocus himself before going on again. The essential is not to be alone, and to remain faithful to this reliable, although often invisible, witness.

Some priests, it is true, never find this help, but that is often because they are expecting one thing from it and it brings them something else. These are people who are too sure of themselves, who will not allow themselves to be answered back, and for whom everything is clear. Or on the other hand they are people whose conception of the spiritual, as of the apostolic life, is limited to instructions and plans that will give them tangible results. Both kinds need to meet with a trial which will touch them at the most sensitive point, and open their minds to a world they do not know. They would discover the world of the Spirit, and would have to acknowledge that it cannot be entered except in that state of simplicity, of surrender, of childlikeness that Our

Lord proclaimed as necessary for the revelation of the mysteries of the Kingdom. Then a spiritual father, if they should meet one at that time, would be able to confirm them in the way, a new way for them, but the only one nevertheless that leads to the unity they are seeking, and which is no other than the way of faith.

*   *   *

In examining the various cases we have brought forward, and all the others it is possible to imagine, two principles emerge throughout. On the one hand, love of the person, of the positive values that he incarnates, and his individual destiny; and on the other hand, a perpetual concern with the divine orientation of that person. In other words, a true director is attached to what is best in a man, in order to submit it to God. He is one who under all circumstances sees further than the difficulties that each person has; he seizes hold of him at his roots, in his movement, in his "dynamic," as we have said. He is sure that the rest will follow. A bad director is one who allows himself to be swamped with his preoccupation over details. He tries to be certain, to foresee everything, as though he did not believe in the action of grace. He wants to have an answer for every question. At what age, he asks, should a decision be taken? What should be said to a married couple who are refusing to have children? These are questions that we must know how to tackle, but in freedom of spirit. Men will always ask such questions; but in the meanwhile, life must go on.

A director should, if possible, be conversant with techniques;

he should study the mentality of the environment to which his ministry assigns him; he should observe the character of the person who is asking his help. There is nothing better. But he should never allow himself to be stifled by techniques, or studies, or observations. It is on the far side of these and beyond, that his assurance lies. Knowing that he cannot be serviceable in all cases and in every environment, he accepts his limitations without making a problem of them. The most important thing for him is that, whatever the field where his ministry is exercised, he should remain the man he is, and should be ceaselessly open to the breath of the Spirit.

CHAPTER FIVE

The Psychology of the Directed

SINCE direction is a dialogue, everything does not depend on the director alone. We must also take account of the other partner. Let us try to say what propensities on the part of the directed will be most likely to hinder or favor the director's activity. It is obviously the director's business to enlighten the directed gradually about the attitude which will allow him to profit from the new relationship that he is wanting to establish.

1. THE FIRST MEETINGS

To enter into the psychology of the directed, it is important to keep in mind the memory of the first contacts: the occasion which led somebody to come and seek you out, and the particular way in which he presented the problem that was worrying him. Without knowing it, he reveals himself wholly in this.

Naturally, there are those who come because they have to. This is usually the case in seminaries and novitiates, where everyone has to have a spiritual father. The person who comes to you is observing an article in the rules, but hardly knows what to expect from it. The personality is asleep and has to be awakened. The situation is often uncomfortable, because the other has absolutely no idea of what to say. He waits to be questioned and answers in monosyllables. He does not understand where your questions are leading. It is not that he is wanting to defend himself; he just does not see what you are trying to get at.

We should not too quickly conclude that there is an absence of desires. Perhaps we shall have to discover a slant through which the personality can manifest itself without even being aware of it. The best thing may be to offer some matter on which it will be led to react. In any case, we must see how the directed behaves with regard to the responsibilities he has, the life he is living, and the group of which he is a member. A retreat can be a valuable time for this assessment; and it will allow us besides to form an impression of the way he prays and lives his religious life. It should be recognized that a prolonged inertia would give cause for grave anxiety. To shake this, it would not be inappropriate to put on a display of sharpness, and talk strongly and loudly, even if we have to make smiling and gentle amends for the somewhat crude reaction we have provoked.

There is the opposite case of the person who comes to see us of his own free will, who talks without embarrassment, but is beside the point and is obviously expecting from direction something quite different from what he should expect. When silence is finally possible, it is a good thing to put the essential question: You are asking me for direction, but what are you expecting from it? Whatever the answer, it will inevitably be significant, so long as we are not taken in by the way in which the person answering expresses himself. The people who talk most confidently are not necessarily those who are most truly giving themselves. They are answering you out of books, or out of their own environment. The important thing to elicit is the kind of answer that will enable you to understand the quality of the soul. It may be lacking in confidence, but it will not be the less true.

Things are simpler when the person approaching us starts from a precise fact. He has come to see us because he cannot extricate himself unaided from the situation in which he is involved, and he begins by telling us about it. His story, the nature of his difficulties and the way in which he is reacting to them will allow us more easily to sum him up. The kind of difficulties he has will give us an idea of the level of human maturity that he has reached.

There are indeed sufferings and sufferings. There is the suffering of the adolescent, enclosed in himself and his problems, irritable, touchy, bringing everything back to himself, in the midst of spasms of generosity and limitless desires. There is the suffering of the man, which he has not himself caused, but is enduring as a result of the encounters and events of life. Both are real, but they cannot be treated in the same way. The personal coefficient which is a mark of the first demands much patience and tact. The other can be handled in a more virile and brotherly fashion. Certainly, it is not rare to meet people of adult years who react to the sufferings of life like the adolescents they have not ceased to be. If you are misled by their appearance and tell them frankly what you think, you will arouse their displeasure: you are just like all the rest; you don't understand me. We meet these reactions in every environment. Religious are equally prone to them. How many are there who are on the look-out for directors who will complacently listen to their little stories and will absolutely agree with them! In the world or in the cloister, they are simply worldlings who are wanting to talk about and receive approval for what they have said and done. You must put your finger on the sore. In which case, either you will have no more visits, or on the other hand you will have gained somebody's trust.

Some people show, by the very way they tell you about the thing that is worrying them, that they expect you to give them a ready-made answer, and instructions that they will merely have to follow. Often these are tranquilizing recipes, which relieve one from the necessity of going deeper or of taking a situation in hand. Just as with the worldlings we were mentioning above, there has to be a fight with these superficial people, ending with the rejection or acceptance of the direction they are asking for. They have to undergo the experience of the sort of dialogue that will call them in question.

These initial contacts are a real passage of arms, and this is necessary so that we can measure one another, accept one another, and locate ourselves on the level of real direction. It involves the exploration of a certain number of domains that the director must have sufficiently clearly in mind to be able to tackle them as he goes along during the first conversations. The answers he gets will put him in a better position to take his bearings afterwards. This is only the first clearing of the ground, but it is important that we should fairly quickly be able to estimate the other person's degree of human and emotional evolution, and at the same time the quality of his spiritual orientation. It would be as well even to distance ourselves sufficiently, or have enough insight, to discover from these first contacts the human fullness of the person we are talking to, even if his appearance allows us to suspect certain disorders or certain faults. We are perhaps face to face with one of those whom we shall never abandon, whatever may happen, because we have at once sensed what seeds he was carrying, or quite simply because we have seen that God was at work in him.

In these first visits, the director must not allow himself to become involved with people who are consulting him about trifles from which all supernatural motive is excluded, or with people who imagine that a priest has "ideas about everything" and that he can be questioned on any subject. A delicate balance, which requires you to receive with kindness people to whom it will do no good to see you again, and whom you will gently have to evict, especially when there is not enough time for you to give to everyone.

Some examples may be given of these opening situations. "For years," somebody says, "I have been thinking about a vocation." "Whether I marry or become a priest," says another, "I feel a kind of passion that I ought not to have." — "I am ill at ease with my superiors, and unhappy in my vocation." — "I am having difficulties in my family and my profession, and here is what I am up against . . ." — "I am engaged, and I don't know whether I am on the right road." — "For years I have been suffering from depression." — "I am bewildered by what my director has said to me."

And should we mention this worldly reason? "I came to see you because I can only confess to a Jesuit." What to say? Somebody else wants to break his spiritual isolation; another would like an answer for his scruples, but of course without letting them go, and wants to find a justification for his conduct, etc. In these first declarations there are conscious and unconscious motives that it is well to bring to light. Not to push away people who are acting from these motives, but because it is indispensable that the contacts to follow should fairly quickly lead them to a point beyond this puerile, worldly, or imperfect stage of development.

It would perhaps be useful to enumerate a certain number of points that a director should encourage the directed to clarify in his presence. Naturally, there is no question of examining him methodically, as though one were holding an inquest. The effect would be disastrous. But in practice, after a little time, we realize that we have discovered the answers to them in one way or another. Here is a summary of such clarifying questions:

1. What does the directed expect from direction? Why is he coming to us especially? What is the dominant motive for his choice? The attraction of a person, the ideas they represent, a sort of sentimental halo, the influence of others, or because it is fashionable? This is one way of finding out how he relates to others.

2. What is the most important problem in his eyes, the one for which he is especially asking our help? Vocation? Difficulties in growing up, or getting along with others? His prayer life? Some choice or other? ... This is the negative side of the question; this is where life is hurting him, and without it he would never have thought of coming to consult us.

3. To find the answer to that special problem, an initial displacement of perspective is often necessary. If someone confesses to difficulties about prayer or chastity, it is a good thing to take soundings in all directions.

In the same way, if he asks a question, it is good to reply by asking others, such as: Why are you asking this question? Have you been asking it for a long time? What happened, what led you to ask it in the first place?

This displacement of perspectives will allow the seeker to get beyond his problem and relate his question to his life as a whole.

It will also enable the director to observe the reaction of the directed to this displacement. Is he surprised? Does he close himself up as if he were being asked indiscreet questions? Does he react intelligently, as a free individual? Perhaps he shows that he is incapable of following our line of thought, and always comes back to the same question, is unable to relax, to launch out boldly and to laugh at himself.

4. As a result of the view that he has been led to take of himself, he raises points that he had never thought of. He becomes conscious of his deficiencies, his failures, and the shortcomings of those who trained him. More than one of the certainties on which his personality was founded, suddenly appears to be fragile. It is important that the effect of our questions should not be to let him dwell on negative points, but should also reveal to him the positive elements of his being. Positively, what have you been wanting? If you were alone and free, what would you wish to do? And even more radically, he must discover a continuity in his existence, an inner force, his "dynamic."

5. A lot of people expect us to question them. It is important to accustom them not to count on our questions, but to talk of their own accord. It is only after we have listened to them for a long time like this that we shall be able to ask the essential question. We shall put it, so to speak, at the turn of the road. Perhaps it will be the one that the other person was secretly afraid of being asked. The trap-question at the inquest. In that case he will have to become conscious of the way in which he is reacting to the question which, if he is willing to accept it, will set him free, because thanks to it he has untied a knot.

It is most desirable that when he has gained confidence, the directed should himself come to the point of unconstrainedly allowing memories or questions to arise in his consciousness and express themselves in words. He will then be giving us his personal way of looking at things, and through that we shall begin to know him. But by a curious effect, he too will begin to know us, and the relationship between him and us will become personal.

6. It is good to observe the angle from which he looks at certain questions—sexual life or religion, for example. His way of speaking about these subjects is much more revealing than the words he says. In regard to the former, a minimum of psychological knowledge is necessary, but above all, much tact is needed to free a person gradually from obsessions or fears that go back to his childhood, and put him at ease with himself and others. As for his prayer life, we must notice how he talks about it, and whether his approach is sentimental, intellectual, or voluntaristic. There is the man who worries about the state of his soul, the one who demands precise instructions about the efforts he should make, the one who refashions the whole world in his prayers, and the one who talks like a book, like his group or his environment. It is only little by little, as a result of our silences and our insistences, that each of these will pass beyond the natural level on which he at first situates his religious life.

The tenor of these questions makes it clear that we shall need more than one conversation to find the answers to them. There will be times when the person we are directing is in danger of being stopped on the way, blocked by some foreboded obstacle. He must not then come up against a wall of indifference in us, but must find that quiet and affectionate reserve which seeks to break down the artifices under which he is taking cover, and will allow him to get to the bottom of himself. In this struggle of which he is the subject, he must feel us to be gently inflexible over essentials. Our firmness will give birth to trust; he knows that he

174

can count on us not to compromise. Or if our attitude disconcerts him, it will bring him to take his stand. As Christ did to those he called, we are offering him a choice at the start of this adventure that will lead him to make many others. The quality of this initial commitment will be, so to speak, the first of the inner purifications that will later make him available to the Holy Spirit.

2. THE QUALITIES OF THE DIRECTED

There are attitudes or qualities that the directed must develop in himself if the enterprise he has begun is to continue, and without them the relationship with his director will become false, or will get bogged down. People often say that they have gained nothing from direction or from a certain director. We have sufficiently discussed the part the director may bear in this failure. But the director cannot do everything. Sometimes he comes up against walls along his way that it is not for him to climb over, or even to go around. They are: lack of intelligence, lack of transparency, and lack of the spirit of faith. What he can at least do is to put the directed in the way of the opposite dispositions.

Intelligence

The director's cross is directing someone who cannot express himself. He is like the patient who tells his doctor he is feeling ill, and with that indication the doctor has to try to determine what is wrong. In order to help someone, a minimum possibility of expression on his side is at least very useful. Certainly, we must not lose patience with his mutism, but must give him enough confidence for him to be able to talk at any rate, and not just answer our questions.

175

There are many people who are not used to analyzing themselves. They have no landmarks in this domain, and so we have to attempt to give them some. Opportunities to do so may be afforded by all kinds of circumstances—certainly in connection with prayer and the inclination one may have for it, but also by the multitude of reactions that are experienced in life and in relationships with others. We have to learn to express our most intimate feelings, so that we may be able from them to judge and discern.

That kind of intelligence is not necessarily speculative; nor is it of the sort that finds pleasure in great supernatural considerations. Still less is it the kind that expresses itself in an abundance of words. The need to examine the quality of our inspiration is often lacking from these grand designs and imposing conversations. As we have said, the director may at first have to put up with this display of ideas or projects, but he must not be taken in by them. His object is to reach intelligence at the point where it is opening to discernment. And it may happen that with people who are very brilliant and very sure of themselves, he will have to be patient for a long, long time, simply because for them the question does not seem to arise.

What he must attempt to develop is a more interior and more penetrating intelligence, keen enough to be able to analyze its states, but not so sufficient as to take pleasure in its analyses. A humble intelligence that respects the facts, and this one first of all: with the best intentions in the world, we may be mistaken. Distrustful of itself, but not tortuous and anxious, it prefers to say things simply as it sees them, allowing itself to be worked on by the question asked, so that it receives new light on it. A progressive intelligence that enters gradually into the reality of its underlying motivations, letting itself be enlightened by action and the reactions of others, and ready at all times to better its understanding.

It will be seen that this intelligence implies much humility and love of God. Its analytical efforts are not an anxious or complacent doubling back on itself, just because it takes its cue from life, from others, from action. It feels comfortable with a solid, natural good sense that puts things in their place and refuses to let itself become entangled with scruples and complications.

Conversations with the director should normally develop this sort of intelligence in the directed. It is his first step towards spiritual discernment and is, as it were, its natural foundation. It presupposes a certain degree of human maturity, because it requires him not to judge his states by his feelings without also being on his guard against the latter. And especially does it demand a readiness to let time go by, not to act or decide impulsively, but to see with lucidity where the lines converge that are drawn by life.

To encourage the development of this sort of intelligence, it may be a good thing to write down what goes on inside oneself. The habit of keeping a spiritual journal is manifestly full of dangers: there is the danger that it may lead to self-complacency, or to a greater attachment to the form than to the matter; some writers even, quite unawares, reproduce what they have read somewhere else, and get into the way of living on fine formulas. For them, spiritual life becomes a world apart, isolating them from reality. The director who advises keeping a journal, or finds that the person he is directing is fond of writing, must be very circumspect. It remains true, nevertheless, that this can be, especially at the beginning, an excellent means of learning to see clearly and forming oneself to a certain subtlety. It is particularly useful if the person who practices it also makes a habit of writing down objectively, at the same time as his own feelings, the opinions or reactions that he provokes. Whatever the procedure undertaken may be, we must in any case develop the intelligence that every man exhibits in ordinary life when he analyses a given situation so as to submit to it and act better. Only in this case the given situation is oneself. Many people live out their situation on the level of instinct, and have never learned to dissociate themselves from it, so as to see and judge it.

Moreover, with time, the analysis becomes shorter and more precise. It helps, not to complicate existence, but to arrive more quickly at the essentials. It accustoms us to precision and honesty, and under these conditions it avoids becoming an empty piece of self-display. We should distrust an intelligence that kept on circling around its own inner states and never achieved a simple attitude. That intelligence would crumble away in analysis of itself.

Let us note for busy directors that mutism is not a sign of lack of intelligence. It may be only a lack of practice, or facility of expression. It may also be the sign of a degree of modesty in a person who does not like to display himself. He may need to be helped out of this state, but it should be respected for its good side. The kind of intelligence that we should wish to find in the directed is asleep, but it exists, and may be original. The opposite quality, too great a facility of speech, above all in this sphere, augurs no good and may not be a sign of special intellectual capacity. It can denote a superficial character, the habit of repeating other people's formulas, and lack of depth of personality. Besides, both mutism and volubility are only the defenses of an individual who is afraid to give himself. Each must be allowed to find his own way: the one will express himself in few words, and the other will have to make great preparations. From this point of view, men and women do not approach the inner world in the same way. Let us help each to attain the goal in his own manner; to be himself and be true.

It is a most painful thing to have to do with someone who quite obviously does not understand. He makes no progress, at least in the direction in which we should like him to. He listens passively, and repeats the same things over and over again, or says nothing at all. Without, if possible, giving him the impression that he is being left on someone else's hands, we should tell him exactly what he ought to do, and try our best to see that after he has received our advice he leaves us in peace. No doubt the peace will be provisional, and very soon we shall have to begin all over again telling him what we have told him a hundred times already. Perhaps, beneath his incapacity to understand our remarks, there is that lack of transparency of which we are about to speak. But the revelation of this absence touches such depths in our being that it is better not to talk of it unless we are absolutely certain; if there is any doubt, we should keep silent.

Transparency

The intelligence which is exercised on itself can maintain its effort only if it is willing to become transparent to the other. This cannot be unless there is a deep renunciation. Without that, however, any real direction falls short or becomes impossible.

Inevitably there will come a time when in this relationship the action of grace will profoundly challenge the one directed. The director himself would prefer to avoid that time, since for him it will be an hour of painful conflict. But nothing good can be accomplished unless both the one and the other are to pass that way.

To emerge from it victorious, the directed must first be prepared to lose everything. We have to repeat concerning him the words of Our Lord: "Unless you become as little children, you shall not enter into the kingdom of heaven." He may have a fine intelligence, superior to that of his spiritual father; he may be a great teacher in Israel; he may in his own field of labors have deep insight and long practice. At this moment, he is no more than a child who must receive everything and must be disjoined from himself, keeping only a prejudice in favor of the one who is helping him to submit himself to God, and that on the points of tenderest feeling.

This, then, is a veritable time of struggle, when with the necessary precautions, but without weakening, the director must say what he believes he has to say, and make the demand which, unless it is conceded, will block all further progress. At this moment the directed has enough enlightenment to decide to follow the director; he knows the one to whom he has entrusted himself; but he has not so much as to be forced to give his consent. At such a moment it is normal for there to come into his mind all the reasons he has for not trusting the other's word. It is a real interior debate, in which all the tangled reasonings only increase his confusion and darkness. To resolve it, he must pass into another order, that of grace; his means, the act of humility of one who puts himself in another's hands, sure of understanding, but only afterwards. When it has been accomplished, this act of freedom finally seals the bond which already exists between director and directed. But it is as painful as childbirth.

The traditional formula says that we must tell our spiritual father everything. This openness is relatively easy at certain periods. It can even seem pleasant on the days when we like to exaggerate our hurts so as to attract more attention. But there comes a time when for one reason or another the confession will not come out. Then, even if we have complete confidence in our director, we have to force ourselves to speak. We are afraid of what the other may think, we are afraid of losing face, or are possessed by the pride that refuses to reveal its inner motivations to somebody else.

This attitude of openness is all the more costly because it is being assumed by an adult. It does not require that he should admit everything with his eyes closed—this would be simply another kind of childishness or wilfulness, and could not last— but that he should allow himself to be judged by the other, to be invaded by this judgment and yet to keep a prejudice in its favor. Even if later on he should come to vary the shades of this judgment or to understand it better, he will first have achieved that preliminary resignation of the spirit through which he denies himself beforehand any position of withdrawal, and accepts the fact of not being for himself his own sole rule of conduct. Only children, fools, or saints, but for very differing motives, would lightly make this sacrifice. It is the hardest thing that can be asked of a man, this renunciation by which he refuses ever to make himself the center of his own inmost heart.

Although this debate does not always assume a dramatic form, the humility which its outcome presupposes is the fundamental attitude that assures the transparency of the heart. It must be formed in the early stages, long before we come up against difficulties which it is vain to try to imagine in advance, and which perhaps we shall never meet. These latter vary so much according to temperaments and conditions of life. But the important thing is that the sacrifice should be accomplished in the interior of the heart. This alone opens us to grace. This alone makes us free. It is the fundamental condition of real dialogue in the relationship of direction. No longer is man alone in his going to God. He has broken his solitude.

If this abnegation did not exist, dialogue could continue only in constrained obedience. It would demand a more and more insupportable effort, and would bring neither peace nor liberation. We should not be deluded by the difficulty that would then make itself felt. It would in no wise be the sign of some greater generosity or the occasion of greater merits; on the contrary, it would bring out into the light that secret pride to which we are refusing to die.

Undoubtedly it can happen, but for other reasons than a self-esteem which will not resign its place, that in the course of its development the relationship should prove to be difficult or impossible. This is the result of differences of points of view or temperament. It is here as with a friendship too lightly entered into: we have to recognize that we were not made for one another. But in this case there is no question of stand-offishness; we have not closed ourselves to the other in face of the demands he has made; it is simply the impossibility of understanding him. No bitterness need remain from this on either side. The necessary separation does not prevent mutual esteem.

It is quite otherwise in the case we have just been considering. If the relationship cannot be established, it is because the disposition which would allow it is absent. When that is lacking, the relationship of direction is impossible with anyone. Or else what is taken for direction is not really such. It is a mixture of friendship, of intellectual exchanges, of pleasant conversations, or even of spiritual considerations. The talks engaged in are simply a sidetrack. In fact there is no direction, because the inner being has not been surrendered in an attitude of self-resignation.

There is a danger of such cases occurring in clerical or religious environments, where people imagine that they know things because they are consulted about them, or speculate about them, or make a profession of being concerned with them. And let us add, so that no one shall feel smug, that the risk is just as often run by a layman, whenever he shuts himself up in his discipline, his technique, or his knowledge, and secretly prides himself on knowing more about things than his director. There is an attitude of perpetual reserve to the counselling he receives, which prevents him from receiving its full impact, or allows him to give the impression that it was already understood. He is unwilling to be touched in that part of his being which he judges to be the best. In the last resort, is it not the absence of willingness to let oneself be hurt that obstructs real relationships between men and prevents love from getting through? Let it be said that the relationship of director and directed does not escape this law, and that when its interplay is fully accepted, it also opens us to love of others.

Since this disposition engages the whole being, it is only with respect and discretion that we may speak to the directed about it. A director who dared to say of anyone that he refused to be open for lack of humility would himself be lacking in respect for others, and would show by the same token that he was more anxious for influence over souls than for their highest good. In fact, tension in an individual can have all the appearance of pride. Who then would be so bold as to pass a final judgment about him? The man before us who is struggling not to surrender himself and sheltering behind his own defenses is nothing more perhaps, in spite of his age, than an adolescent who is afraid to let go of the certainties that he has managed to acquire for living, and is filled with panic in face of an adventure the issue of which seems to him so uncertain. He finds reassurance in remaining rigid, and enclosing himself in austere practices. And all that with the best faith in the world. What is quite certain, nevertheless, is that he is going round in circles and is not finding peace. Or the peace he says he has is only a silence brutally imposed on all his interior objections. This we can easily see. But once again, we must not judge. So long as he is coming to us, we should receive him with kindness, while still holding firm. One day perhaps, we shall have the joy of seeing this stubborn will bend, and open itself through humility to love. Then we shall all the more completely share his joy because the time of waiting was so long. But perhaps also his absences may lengthen, until at last we are not seeing him any more. We shall not judge him, or think of him as lost. God has other means than ours of bringing him to Himself.

A Spirit of Faith

The transparency which is the foundation of all real relationships requires in the case of direction a great spirit of faith on the part of the directed. No doubt that spirit of faith is at first to be understood in the natural sense of the word, inasmuch as one person puts his faith in another. There must be an establishment of trust between the two, and trust includes, as it normally should, all kinds of natural feelings. Do not let us try to disentangle them too soon, or ask the one we are directing too early to see clearly into himself. Time will do its work. It will be enough if in this entanglement we ourselves are not made fools of.

But whatever the feelings which give birth to the relationship, it cannot long be maintained unless the directed, without being too concerned at first with human sentiments, founds it on a supernatural faith. At certain times this faith is naked, and rests only on the once admitted need of direction. But whatever its echoes may be in the natural order, it is from the beginning what it will be afterwards: an adherence to the word of Christ, and a means of binding ourselves to the mystery of the Church in our innermost beings. The relationship that it engenders fulfills in the secret places of the soul the mystery of the Church visible and invisible, the mystery of the Christ-man.

The more this incipient relationship becomes a bond between adults, the more it is established in faith. It is just at the moment when we might be tempted to say it was no longer useful, because a person has become capable of managing on his own, that it bears its fruit. It becomes a communion of souls, a confirmation in the work of the Holy Spirit, a means of profound acquiescence in the Spirit's will. Even if it has overtones of friendship, it preserves that basis of respect which leads those who have become united in this way to go beyond appearances and to see themselves in the universal mystery of Christ and of the Church. Then director and directed, as in all spiritual communication, give and receive in turn. It is the beginning of a true dialogue in the Holy Spirit. It is also a common presence at a veritable action of God in the hearts of both. Direction is not a means of insight into oneself or an aid in taking decisions, but the expression of a common desire to seek and accomplish God's will in the world. Its aim is truly the building of the Kingdom of God, as we like to say in these days, giving the word the fullness of meaning that it had for St. Paul.

A Spirit of Simplicity

Some people feel uneasy in the presence of this relationship. They do not see the need for it, or else they are aware of its dangers, and consider that it is better to approach God without its help. They judge their attitude to be more in conformity with the simplicity of the Gospel, and quote in support of their arguments the words and example of St. Thérèse de l'Enfant Jésus. "Directors," she wrote in one of her letters, "help us to advance in perfection by making us do a great number of acts of virtue, and they are right; but my director, who is Jesus, does not teach me to count my acts, but shows me that I must do everything out of love, and refuse Him nothing . . ."

Rather than using them as arguments against direction, let those who take their stand on these texts endeavor to practice the exercise they indicate, in the midst of every one of their actions. If they find no difficulty in this, and if they have no need of counsel to improve themselves in it, they will soon come to see that their desire to dwell unceasingly in the presence of God and to refer every action and thought to him will produce in them the purification and the discernment of their intentions that the early ascetics of the Church sought in spiritual direction. They will be making in another form the discovery of that sifting of the thoughts in the frequent recollection of the Lord Jesus which was counselled by the Fathers. If they then go forward in peace, seeing lucidly what they are doing against God and confessing it, if they live heedful of what is required of them by the duties of their station and in contacts with others, they are in that reality towards which direction leads. Let them not be anxious, but serve God in peace. If they do not succeed in this manner of conduct, or grow weary in it, the facts will reveal the need they have of spiritual help.

But there are others whose simplicity, more evident to themselves than to those about them, may be only a means of hiding their reluctance to be open or their fears of commitment. They claim to possess the spirit of childhood, but they have lost its candor and delicacy and seem to have kept only its obstinacy and simple-mindedness. They should at least try to objectify in the course of a discussion the motives for their repugnance, to see whether it comes from a concern for fidelity to the Gospel or from the fear of self-revelation. This would be a great advantage for them, and also for the quality of the influence they exercise over others.

They would then discover that this relationship which they thought so complicated is simpler than they imagined. They would discover, thanks to the efforts they had made, a certain quality of relationship of which their past experience had perhaps given them no idea. They would learn through it, not only how to love God a little more, but to begin to love their fellow men.

Conclusion

THERE are two points which we have made in this book which will allow us better to place direction: among human activities it is of an order apart, that of the Spirit; in the life of the Church, it cannot be enclosed in preëstablished categories, because it is a charisma. On the one hand, it does not contradict human wisdom but goes beyond it, as grace surpasses nature; on the other, it does not fit into any institution of the Church, although it is in no way independent of it. By way of conclusion, let us return with some emphasis to these two points.

The recent development of the knowledge and techniques of psychology, like that of the knowledge of the universe, has been so astonishing that we find it difficult to think of any human activity, even of a religious order, that can escape its explanations or its laws. And what remains obscure today, progress will clarify tomorrow. Faced with this mentality, which is that of our time and in which he participates, the spiritual director remains the witness of an order irreducible to those of which science yields us the secrets. Without denying the dynamism of the individual or the group, he believes in that of grace. As Christ did to Nicodemus, who was a teacher in Israel, he speaks of it as a fact: "We bear witness to that we have seen" (Jn. 3, 11).

He does not try to give proofs, because he sees its self-evident effects. "That which is born of the Spirit is spirit. . . . The wind blows where it wills, and you hear the sound of it, but you do not know whence it comes or whither it goes; so it is with every one who is born of he Spirit" (Jn. 3, 6. 8). The world of the operations of Spirit is as solid for him as that of visible reality.

It is not that he is ignorant of psychology or that he expects nothing from its researches. He does not succumb to the temptation of many believers, who react with a reflex of fear to a science which is likewise tempted to be enclosed and self-sufficient. On the contrary, he knows that all scientific progress helps him to orient himself better, and to define the boundaries of his own activity. Even more, he is persuaded that this supernatural world, of which he affirms the primacy, cannot be separated from nature. As we have many times repeated in this work, the supernatural penetrates nature and invades it from all sides. The action of grace, like "The Hidden Presence of Christ" in the world,[1] is so closely interwoven wth the series of human events that it is difficult to dissociate it from them.

The single object of his function is to develop the insight of faith, which, in the midst of human affairs, discovers the signs of God and becomes sensitive to them. This discovery obeys other laws than those of scientific research: it is a work of humility of heart and resignation of spirit. A man who does not believe in these Gospel values forbids himself entry into that new world. He is like a blind man hearing colors talked about, but not knowing what they mean.

So it is that the director, a witness in the visible world to the

[1] The title of one of Cardinal Newman's sermons. See *Cardinal Newman's Best Plain Sermons*, London and New York, 1965, pp. 97–108.

world invisible, is both modest and independent. Modest in that he does not think he knows everything and can manage everything himself. Modest also because he accepts the contributions of science, respects them, and as far as possible acquaints himself with them.

But while he admires and esteems the values of the world, he remains independent. He knows that all the sciences in the world and the whole of human progress will not avail to bring into being a supernatural love; he knows, too, that eventually there is a point when science has nothing to say when confronted with the phenomenon of human love. "From all bodies and spirits," wrote Pascal in his *Pensées,* "there cannot be drawn forth an impulse of true charity; that is impossible, of another order, supernatural." Only, in contrast to Pascal, the spiritual director is more aware, as are his contemporaries, of the connections of the three orders and their unity in the great sweep of human evolution, than he is concerned with distinctions which fail to make their relatedness apparent.

We have said that a second important point is to preserve the originality of direction in the complex activity of the Church. Just as there are many priests today who, in their anxiety not to lose contact with the world, give it so much of their attention that they can see nothing else, there are others so concerned to confine everything within ecclesiastical structures that they would like to obliterate or ignore what does not come into that setting. This is a very understandable apostolic kink, but it is a kink just the same. They are like those educators who are so enamored of their principles that they apply them even when it stops the development of the personalities for which they were originally established. So here is one of the aspects of direction that this book has striven to make clear at every turn: it belongs in the order of charismas which are, within the unity of the Church, the manifestation of the freedom of the Spirit.

Priests have in all ages tended to reject from their perspectives anything that does not fit into their schemes or submit to their action. The danger is as manifest today as in other times. The unity of which we sometimes dream is rather that of an organization with definite characteristics and precise directives than the living unity of the Body which ceaselessly grows out of its inner strength, inspired by the unforeseeable creations of the Spirit. Our impatience when we are confronted with the fact of spiritual direction, apart from the irritating caricatures we are occasionally given of it and which justify our censure, is one of the multitudinous expressions of this tendency to reject whatever will not allow itself to be reduced to our logic. Direction is not indeed in the service of any movement. In this connection as in all, we must beware of seeking to imprison the dynamism of the Spirit.

It is a charisma, as we have often said; that is, an absolutely gratuitous gift that the Holy Spirit makes to whom He wills. We might prefer it to be an art that we could master, and the first thing to recognize is that it is not. The Master is the Holy Spirit, whose gifts are given as they are intended to be given. This does not mean that we have to wait passively to be pushed into action. God expects us to make ourselves ready for his gifts. Moreover, in this charisma, everyone receives his own measure and his particular way of exercising it. The danger appears at the moment when we no longer admit the ascendancy and independence of the Spirit, and want to regulate things as we like. As if direction could happen of its own accord, and we only needed a good course of lectures to become good directors. It is at the moment when it is institutionalized and becomes an examination subject that the reality of direction is most likely to be degraded.

Possibly as he closes this book the reader may feel diappointed. Is he any further forward after reading it than he was before? Can he give a clear definition of direction? He wanted an easily handled guide and precise instructions, and he has heard instead about a mysterious world which it is unwise to enter unless one has the gift. He is tempted to think that this is an easy explanation.

In fact, here as in all living realities, he is expected to find his own place. It is as an intelligent servant, and not under the impulse of grace acting without an effort on his part, that he must exercise this function for which his aptitude has been recognized. Since he is dealing, not with inert matter but with living and free individuals, he cannot hope to be effective in this world of personal relationships and mutual dependences unless he accepts himself first of all. He has to be a man. He cannot get out of it at lesser cost. More deeply, as a man, he must know that he is set on other ends than those humanity affords. His inner law is that of the Spirit which, within the reality of the present Church, is making ready the eternal Bride of Christ.

And so direction becomes an experience on either side which binds us to the Church and has universal value. Addressing itself to the individual, it does not throw him back on himself. If it did, the best would become the worst, and the director would prove to be more of a hindrance than a help. But that happens only to those who have not understood the very simple saying of Father Surin which sums it all up.

"What does the direction of souls consist in?"

"In forming Christ in them, according to the words, 'until Christ be formed in us' " (see Gal. 4, 19).